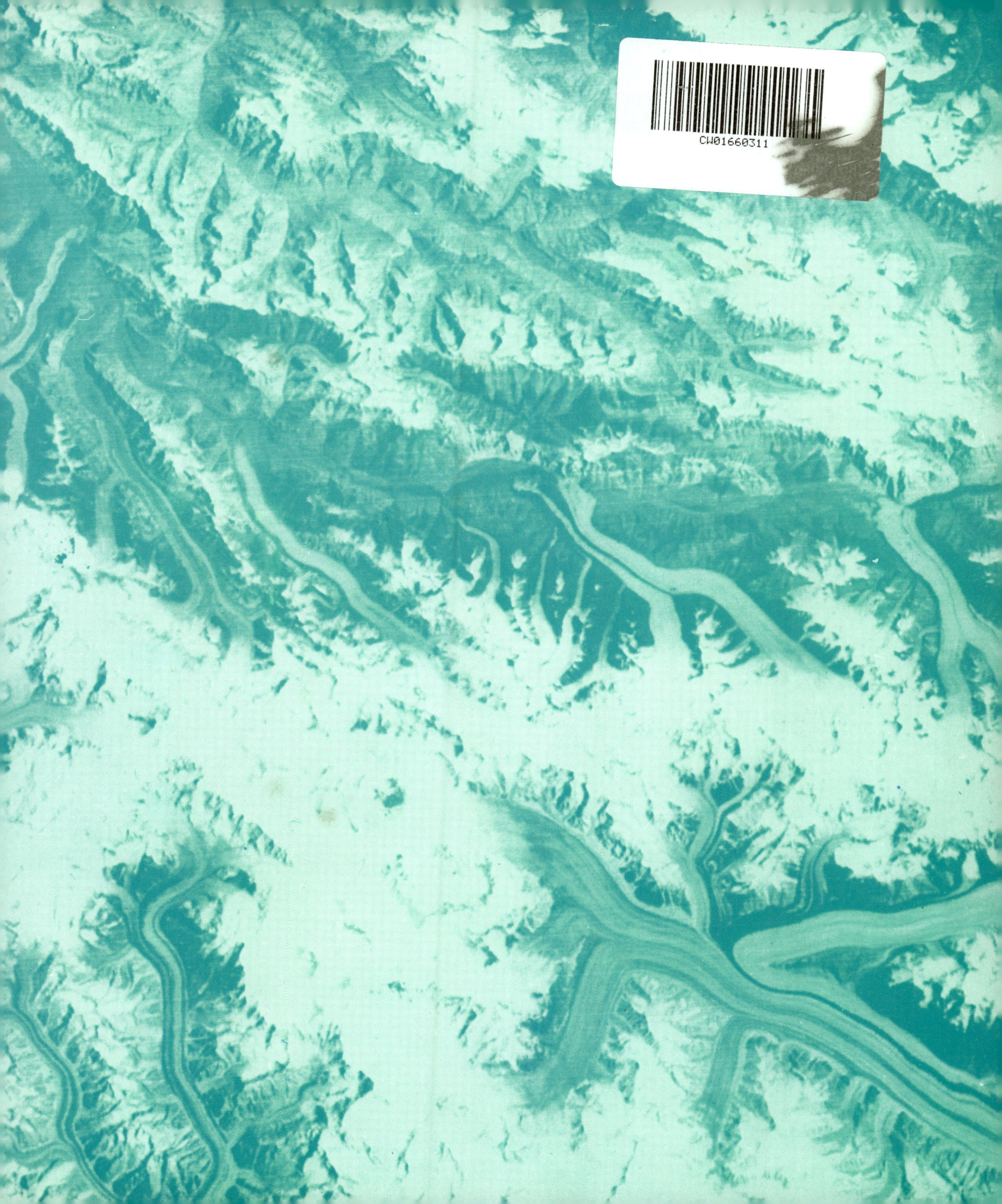

Deep in the heart of the Himalaya, they have a legend about a high and holy mountain. From its summit your shadow is cast across the land beneath, revealing to you the way you should go, showing you yourself, as in a dream.

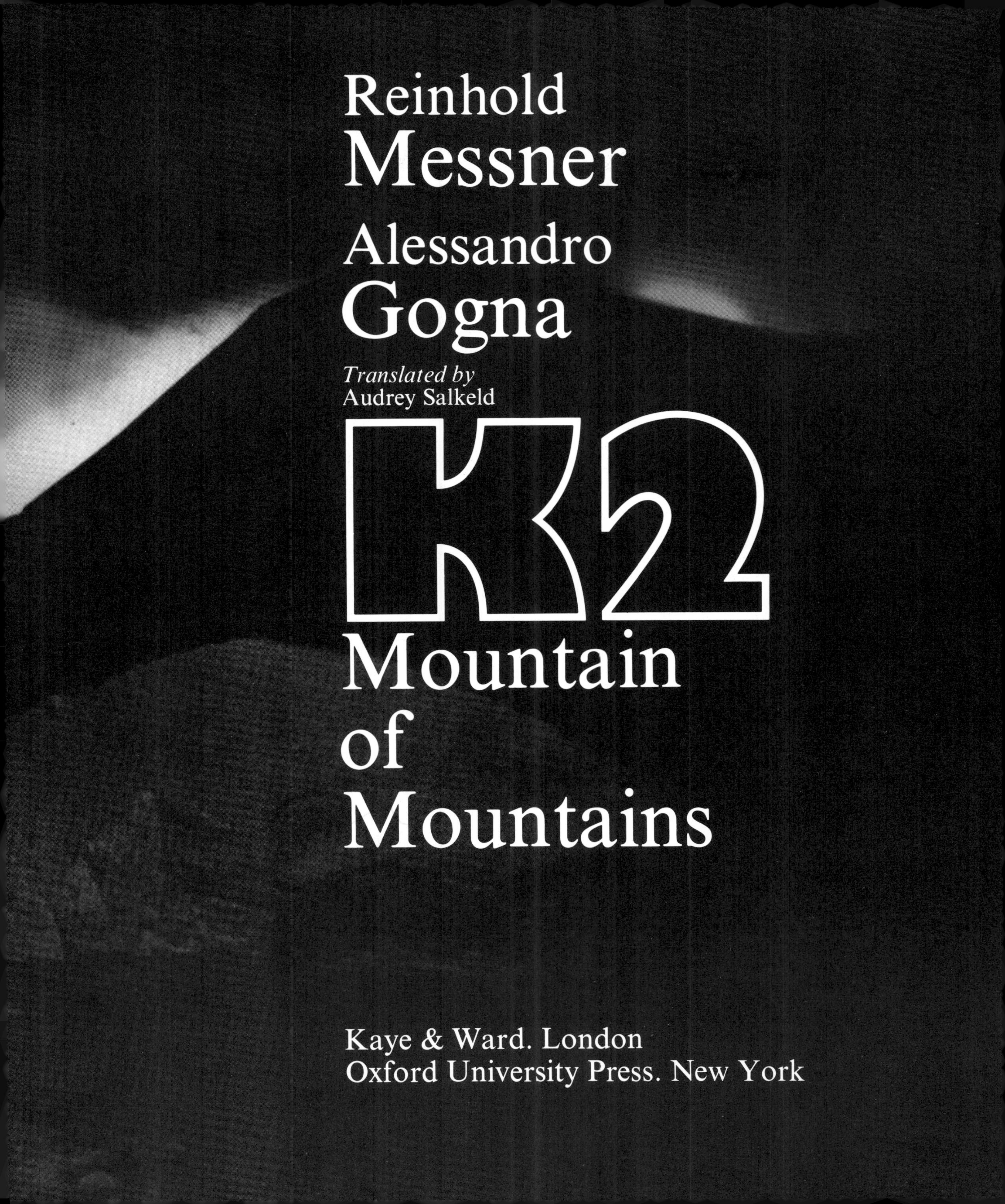

Reinhold
Messner

Alessandro
Gogna

Translated by
Audrey Salkeld

K2
Mountain of Mountains

Kaye & Ward. London
Oxford University Press. New York

Dustjacket: Aerial picture of K2 from the west. (photograph: Dianne Roberts)	*It was a mountain unbelievably higher than anything I had imagined, and I was only a few miles from its base, so that I could realize its height to the full.* *I knew not what mountain it was; but I found afterwards that it was no other than K2.* (Sir Francis Younghusband)
Front endpaper: Satellite picture of Central Karakorum. (IBM)	*Whether the Karakorum constitutes a system of mountains in itself or whether it forms an integral part of the Himalaya is not very clear. But since the geographical nomenclature of the great mountain ranges of the world is for the most part conventional it is usual to regard the Karakorum as one of the great orographical units of the Himalayan chain, occupying a position comparable to that of the Bernese Alps vis-à-vis the Alpine system. The Karakorum is, moreover, the northern most portion of the Himalaya, its latitude being roughly the same as that of Gibralter.* (Ardito Desio)
Reverse front endpaper: K2 from the north-east. (photograph: Vittorio Sella)	*K2 – the ultimate, the most inspired expression the force of mountain-building has produced on our planet.* (Günther Oskar Dyhrenfurth)
Pages 2/3: The 1978 American rope just below the summit. (photograph: Robert Schaller)	*At 5.20 in the afternoon we set foot on the highest point. . . . At long last Americans had made it. Not Lou Reichardt and Jim Wickwire, nor yet Jim Whittaker, nor the other team members. Just Americans.* (James Wickwire)
Reverse rear endpaper: K2 from the south.	
Rear endpaper: Godwin–Austen sketch with K2 upper left. (photograph: Vittorio Sella)	*This peak was first observed in 1856 by Montgomerie, from a high point in Kashmir, to the south. He named it Mount Godwin–Austen in commemoration of that officer's brilliant work in executing the first glacier survey in this forbidding region. But the Indian Survey is over modest and will not accept personal names: so it remains K2, just as in Montgomerie's original fieldbook.* (Tom Longstaff)

First published in Great Britain by
Kaye & Ward Ltd
The Windmill Press
Kingswood, Tadworth, Surrey
1981
First published in the USA by
Oxford University Press Inc.
200 Madison Avenue, New York, N.Y. 10016
1981

Title of the original German edition:
K2 BERG DER BERGE

ISBN 0 7182 3940 7 (Great Britain)
ISBN 0–19–520253–8 (USA)

Library of Congress Catalog Card No. 80–84676 (USA)

Printed in Great Britain by Butler and Tanner Ltd

Filmset by Hunter-James/MS Filmsetting Ltd

Passages in quotation marks and italics are quotations from diaries of expedition members, or from actual historical publications, etc; see also sources of reference page 176.

The K2-Expedition was partly sponsored by the BLV Verlagsgesellschaft. All members promised to put their diaries and pictures at the disposal of the expedition book.
Reinhold Messner with his experience as a writer has edited the material and tried to be fair to all participants.

A Dream, a Team, an Adventure

We both share the same ideas; Reinhold had the enthusiasm, the endurance. (Alessandro Gogna)

Ever since I first stood at its foot in 1975, K2 has fascinated me. In 1979 I organised an expedition there with the object of giving a few younger climbers an opportunity to take part. Eight of us set off from Europe in May. Then our doctor Ursula Grether had to be helicoptered back; it was a bitter blow for the expedition, even though Robert Schauer was able to take over the medical duties. And it meant more responsibility for me. It had been my own idea to attempt K2, I made all the plans, supplied most of the finance and chose the team.

Alessandro (Sandro) Gogna I invited because I like him. He and I are the same kind of person; I need him – although I could never tell him that. He is one of those people who knows what death is about, and loves the world. People and nature are what really matter to him. Then there were Michl Dacher and Friedl Mutschlechner, both rather alike in their directness and their total lack of pretension. I feel an affinity with them based on the fact that we have shared climbs in high places.

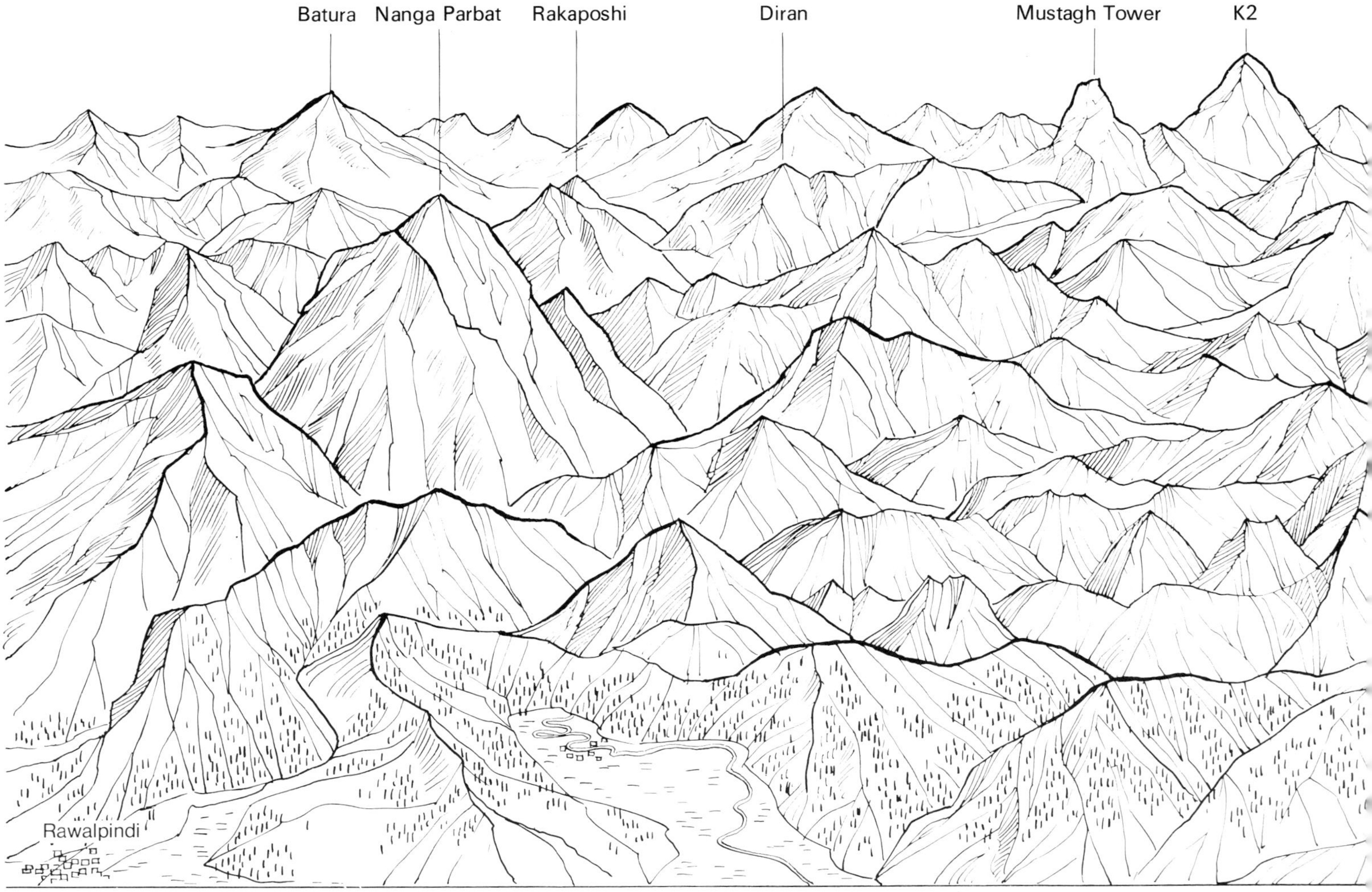

Fortunately times have changed since alpinists were obliged to concentrate their efforts solely on planting some bit of national bunting on one summit or another (Reinhold Messner)

I invited Renato Casarotto because I believed him at the time to be one of the ablest European climbers; and Robert Schauer because he had demonstrated endurance and commitment during our Everest climb. As it turned out, our K2 adventure was to prove harder than the Everest climb. Six weeks after the start of the expedition I wrote in my diary: 'I ought not to have brought along anyone for their climbing merit alone.' The insight came too late. It was my mistake and I had to answer for it. I felt let down by Robert on a personal level, by Renato as a climber.

So, in the same way that we undertook the expedition as a team, together we fashioned this book. We wanted to set down our experience, hard and brutal as it was at times, in words and pictures. Each gave what he was prepared to give: Sandro his diary, Friedl, Renato and Michl a few pictures, Joachim (Jochen) Hoelzgen, who came as a journalist but became a full member of the expedition, his historical notes on K2.

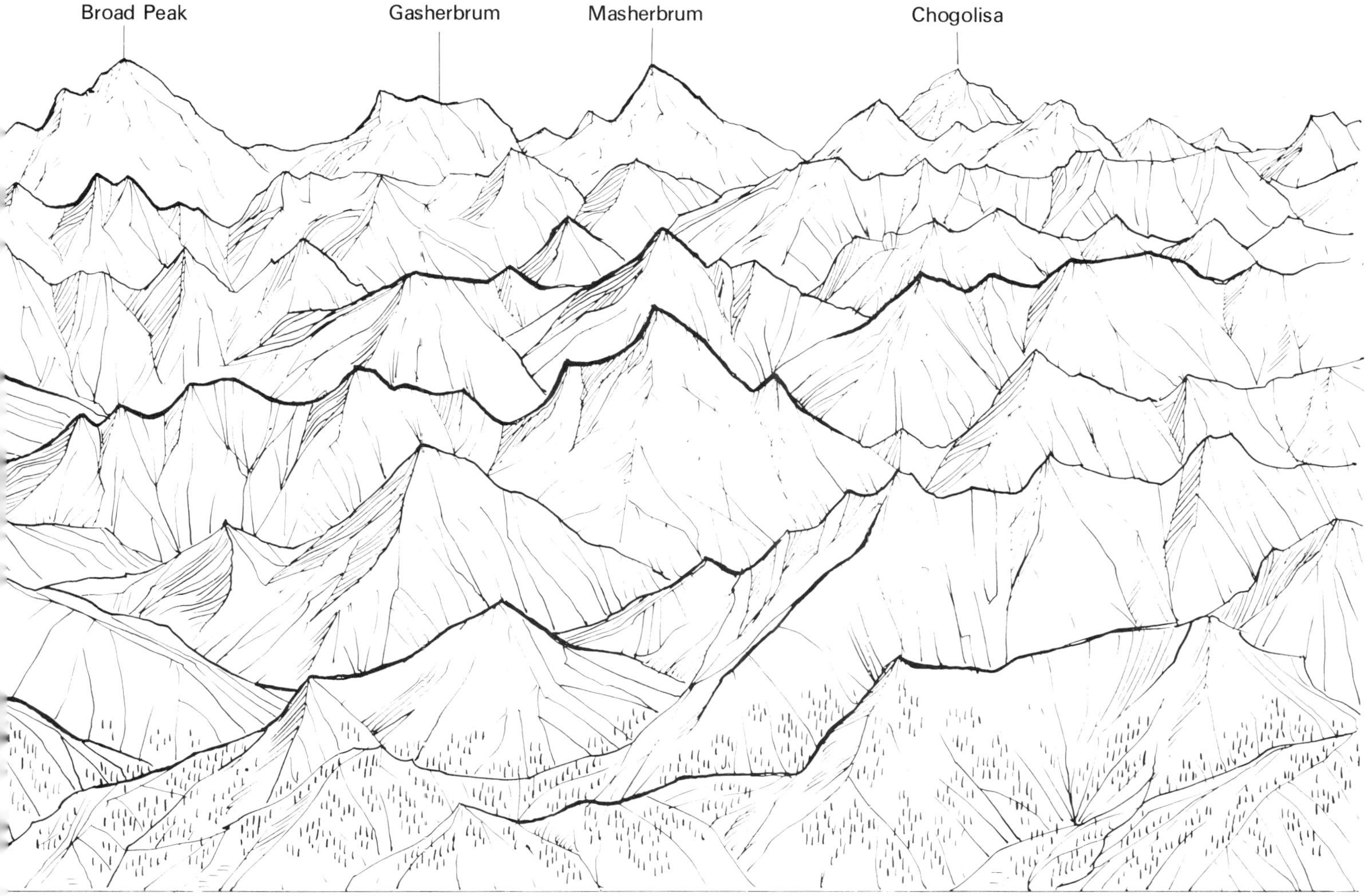

Dreams into Reality

Nine Months' Gestation

I have divided the Heavens, I have cleft the Horizon, I have traversed the Earth upon his footsteps. The mighty Khu taketh possession of me and carrieth me away, because, behold, I am provided with his magical words for millions of years. . . .
(Old Egyptian Book of the Dead)

Joachim Hoelzgen

There is this little house in the middle of the woods with the curious name 'The Black Fairies', and it was right by there, whilst running, that I suddenly and painfully strained a ligament in my ankle at the beginning of September 1978. I felt very bitter about it; nothing quite so stupid had ever happened to me before and I was utterly convinced that I hadn't stepped awkwardly or anything. At the time I cursed those 'Black Fairies' for the mischief, and almost immediately felt an extraordinary pain in my neck and was unable to move it properly.

Reinhold and I had already agreed the exact date for our departure for K2. The waiting period had begun, and for me this proved to be a painful gestation.

It is now mid-April and I am in the eighth month. I take advantage of my acquaintance with the director of the Bioclinic in Milan to try and find the cause and nature of all my troubles. Professor Montemagno treats his patients with chirotherapy, acupuncture and other natural methods. I am waiting, stretched out, on his examination couch. He senses that I am very tense; his fingers have a magic touch. He talks to me about climbing and tells me of an experience he came upon whilst reading a book by an Indian author, an experience that transcends time and allows consciousness of one's self only – in one supreme moment, at the climax, when one's effort and determination fuse into a single entity. I am touched that anyone like him should speak of something which he hasn't really experienced himself, and yet come so near to the truth – a truth which I myself do know. But I merely nod and avoid a discussion that might lead us too far and lure me into giving too much of myself away. The secret must remain hidden. The treatment is unsuccessful. However, when the time comes to depart for K2, my pains disappear as mysteriously as they came. I scarcely notice it, but then quickly others, stronger than before, take their place. I have come full-term, the 'child' is ready to be born. Like a mother-to-be, I am ready.

The journey is a long one, and as purifying as a pilgrimage. During this time the other five expedition members seem to me to be superior, although we are all equally good climbers. The only two with whom I feel at ease are Joachim, a journalist with the news magazine *Der Spiegel*, and Terry, who is our Pakistani Liaison Officer.

There is also one woman. It hits me in a dream just how pretty a young blonde can be. In my dream she is washing her hair. When she is ready, she comes towards me, but I feel incapable of proving my manhood to her. I feel cheap and dirty. I hurry away and manage to reach a room in the clinic where there are two patients asleep. I can't seem to find the wash-basin; I want to wash my penis. The girl is at the door, wanting to come in. I haven't much time. I shout to her to wait. I don't want her to see me like this. But already her smiling face appears around the door. Behind her stands Professor Montemagno, he radiates calm and security, and I no longer feel any shame in front of either of them.

The pain in my neck has made it clear to me that I ought never to twist round, otherwise I will miscarry. But there won't be an abortion. Mother and child will die together in the great clinic of Nature, or will live together in the world outside.

9 May
Voice on the Telephone

'. . . I called you just to say how much of a friend you have always been to me – more than that, you have been the only one who has really understood, and who has had the courage to do things your own way. I wanted to say I would have liked to be with you. Perhaps we'll see each other there. Perhaps now, after so many years of waiting, I, too, will at last get to Asia. For you, I'm sure this will be the most important climb of your life; I'm certain of it. Perhaps you will be the only one of them to get up, you on your own. It will be hard, of course, but I'm convinced you'll do it. I'll follow you, I'll be there. Now you must go. . . .'

12 May
Death is a Part of Life

You must leave now, take what you need, you think will last,
But whatever you wish to keep, you better grab it fast.
Yonder stands your orphan with his gun,
Crying like a fire in the sun.
Look out the saints are comin' through,
And it's all over now, Baby Blue.'
(Bob Dylan)

At 23.00 hours I pick up Michl Dacher from the main railway station in Milan. Robert Schauer arrived early in the morning, also by train. I look up at the moon; it is full. I am happy and enthusiastic at the prospect of this expedition. All the signs are good. We should achieve something. There follows the usual bivouac at my house. Friends lying all over the floor, waiting for morning.

At Linate Airport I get very emotional at one point. While all the familiar faces of the pressmen try and pick up the latest titbits or detect the first signs of disagreements, I concentrate on my wife, Nella. When we get to the police check and I find myself alone in the sea of passengers, cut off from Nella and all the others, including Aldo and Marina Anghileri who arrived at the last minute, my throat suddenly tightens. I realise how attached I am to my friends, how much I love my wife, and am quite overcome. But I also feel an inward rush of freedom, even when for an instant I suddenly imagine I am dead and about to be buried.

Sitting in the plane, I can't help thinking how empty the flat must seem without me. My father would most likely come to Milan to look for photos and other mementos of me. Nella wouldn't be difficult and would give him everything he wanted. And perhaps my father would be surprised at her generosity and even conclude that Nella doesn't really love me. It was picturing how Nella sometimes cries when she thinks about me that gives rise to these morbid, yet seductive fantasies. When we land at Fiumicino I again have a premonition of death, which shakes me even more.

In Fiumicino we are again at the centre of a milling crowd. Someone asks me if we are baseball players. 'Yes', I reply and he is glad that he figured it right. The plane from Munich, with Reinhold and our doctor, Ursula Grether, aboard, is late. When it arrives it is immediately besieged by television people and journalists. Reinhold is in fine form. He talks about his climbing and his mental balance. He winds up his masterly and spellbinding performance by saying that death is a part of life. Everyone gets very excited.

But Renato Casarotto remarks shrewdly, 'They don't really understand what Reinhold has been saying because it doesn't really concern them at all.'

13 May
Strange Land

Rawalpindi is without doubt the most horrible town in Pakistan, even the Pakistanis say that. But they set against it that the capital city, Islamabad, only nine miles away, is much more beautiful and attractive.

Unfortunately we Europeans cannot share their viewpoint. To me, Islamabad seems seedy and oppressive. 'Pindi', as Rawalpindi is popularly known, is a dusty business centre without any historical buildings. The bazaar and the main street, the Murree Road, are very lively, but to anyone who knows the bazaars of other oriental towns, this one seems to lack atmosphere. People only sell what they need in their day-to-day life, and these articles are predominantly plastic. There is not a single picturesque corner, only bustle and noise and a lot of beggars.

14 May
Legal Formalities

Despite everything I am quite happy. It is not the same atmosphere as on my earlier expeditions. I am just a bit fed up because I feel somewhat purposeless. It may be that I haven't yet had the opportunity of showing myself to my best advantage. But that's my usual problem. One day I must come to terms with the fact that in life it is only important to be myself. Renato, Friedl and I are in a room signing thousands of expedition postcards. It is hot outside. To stick the postage stamps on we dip napkins in water. The silence is broken by Renato, who tells us – I'm not sure what led up to it – of a journey from San Candidò to Merano and back during his time in the army. I mentioned my military service as well, with the Scuola Alpina in Moena.
'It sounds as if you could easily have signed on for longer,' said Friedl, 'there was a Major in Aosta who wanted me to.'
'Did you give him cause for hope?'
'Far from it! I never said a thing about it. All I wanted was to get home quickly. Once, we were in the Grigna for a climbing course and they even sent a woman to my room!'
'You're kidding?' Renato and I echo in chorus.
'I had been up the Nibbio and wanted to rest in my room. There was a knock on the door. "Come in!" There was this young girl and she drapes herself around my neck. My superiors had thought that because of the language difficulty, I was having trouble finding a girl. At that time I knew even less Italian than I do now. But all *I* wanted was to climb, nothing more. I counted the days till I could be in Bruneck again – not a thought for girls! So I get up from bed and throw the girl out. "Go away!" Then I clump down the stairs, go to the bar and pour five *grappas* down my throat, and then another five. I was completely plastered, couldn't stand up, but I was even madder than before, and when my superiors came in I yelled at them, "If you think you can get round me like this, you're very much mistaken!" '
On this expedition, we too have our military brass. Mohammed Tahir, whom we call Terry, is our Liaison Officer and he holds the rank of Major. He is a military judge, and lives in Quetta, Baluchistan. His grandparents were Afghani, or to be more exact, Uzbek. Terry is very nice and speaks good English. He has a proud bearing, jet black eyes, and a thick, well-groomed beard. Because of the language problem and because Terry is such an engaging personality, much of the conversation within the group is frequently conducted in English. It pleases him that not only Reinhold and Ursula – his friends from last year when Reinhold climbed Nanga Parbat on his own – but I, too, am familiar with Pakistani food.

Friedl Mutschlechner

15 May
An Insult, a Kiss, an Invitation

In a dream I see Ursula coming towards me. She kisses me gently. Reinhold is there and I'm very worried he will get angry and forbid it. Nothing happens. It is a beautiful, tender kiss and I want to return it – then I spot two vampire teeth and the kiss becomes torture.
(Alessandro Gogna)

One day Ursula chides me for taking everything so seriously. She says I seldom laugh. But it is hard to talk in English sub-titles. It is this language barrier that separates us. She is a girl with many qualities: she is intelligent, intuitive, and has the gift of being able to spread happiness. It grieves me that I cannot communicate with her properly and that I must seem practically an idiot to her. It is almost as if I were shy of her. As if deep down I felt I had not yet earned her proximity, was unworthy of emotional contact with one who is the visible representative of that invisible woman who, in my inmost heart, I have condemned to destitution, to be a beggar-woman. She arouses in me images of disturbing sensuality, an orgy of women, countless women, as a contrast to that wretched woman in utter distress.

A spacious room, furnished in the western style and decorated with a valuable carpet and Chinese prints; fifteen chairs arranged along the walls, a large, clear area in the middle: this is the setting for the evening meal, to which we have been invited by Hassan Ali Reza, a very agreeable friend of Terry's. Hassan's mother, a beautiful, educated woman welcomes us with a radiant smile. She wears a sari. His father, Hassan Abdul Kalik, an Iranian, a retired General, appears rather more formal, but even so seems proud to be able to welcome such distinguished foreign visitors into his house. The conversation is lively. A last evening of civilisation. Tomorrow, Robert and I set off for Skardu.

16 May
Our own particular Problem

I have been feeling slightly under the weather for days; I am weak and have diarrhoea. I don't let myself get too alarmed, although inevitably I find myself asking whether I'll be able to stay healthy or not. Nevertheless I am calm. By 'calm' I mean that I'm pleased enough with myself; but not yet content through and through. Many times we think the C-130 will never take off. When we do finally get away, I cannot believe the gigantic massif of Nanga Parbat outside the tinted cabin windows. The Hercules is not the sort of plane from which to take photographs, but nevertheless, the Japanese climbers who are sharing our flight, take great pains to snap everything.
The first thing we do in Skardu is to visit the Commissioner; he is like the Mayor of the town. We discuss porters and jeeps. In a cordial atmosphere, augmented by several cups of good tea, we even discuss why we climb mountains. It is obvious we don't do it for money. I assert that it is a kind of craft; Robert says what a splendid thing it is to find one's own way by oneself.
'But why in this wilderness? Why not where there are some other people, some life?'
'Unfortunately that's how it is on an expedition. It's not permanent. We do also enjoy climbing alpine summits with our families.' I can read deep disbelief in the eyes of the man opposite and realise in my heart that I've lied. The cosy family picnic scene doesn't really fit a father like me!
Outside the light is transparently clear and there is a pleasant, stiff, breeze blowing. We take our leave.
Below Skardu Fort, the Indus flows sluggishly across a sandy, desert-like

Alessandro Gogna

plain. It carries less water at this time of year. Brown mountains rise against a tired sky. We wander through the town. In the bazaar, the traders squat in their little booths. One of them smokes a hookah; they wait for closing time. Women crouch amongst the plants. Some porters from the neighbouring villages come up to us and ask if we are the Italians who want to go to K2. They offer their services.
Talking with Robert, I find myself repeating an old argument, 'Asia is divided into two halves – the Hindu-Buddhist half and the World of Islam. Maybe it's always easier to make friends with the neighbours of neighbours, but personally I had much less trouble feeling at home in Nepal and India, than in Pakistan or Iran, amongst all the hypocrisy, falsehood and servility.' But the Mohammedans, too, are an extension of ourselves, their culture and religion is very like our own. The problem lies with us if we find them unpleasing. Not that I'm in favour of universal love and peace, all that 'stick-flowers-in-your-guns' rubbish. That, to me, is too glib; decadent, hippy mumbo-jumbo.
It is part of my nature that I often have to maintain a certain detachment from people, that sometimes I hate everyone. To hell with this conversation! Better perhaps the peace in this valley which lies at 2300 metres above sea level.
The tranquillity here is very enviable. It is unbroken and even accentuated by the regular call to prayer of the Muezzin over the loud-speaker.
There are many Hunzas here in Skardu, the main town of Baltistan. They are happy to find work with expeditions. Fine, proud figures of men, they stand out amongst the more inconspicuous Baltis. One of them asked whether we knew that the successful 1954 Italian expedition employed solely Hunza porters for high-level work, naming in particular the celebrated Mahdi. However, we want to do without high-level porters at all.

18 and 19 May
Selection

In the quiet of my room in the Hotel Baltoro a little nocturnal drama is being played out. The hours seem to drag because I have the impression that I'm lying here awake. Actually I'm not awake, I'm dreaming that I'm stuck between four or five expedition boxes and can't get out. When I do wake up, I'm in a foul humour. I go into breakfast without saying 'Good Morning' to anyone. In the dining room Hadji Ahmad Khan, boss of *Karakorum Travel* is waiting for me. His is a jeep and transport business, as diverse and far-reaching as it is confused and rapacious. By the end of our conversation I am feeling better.
I ask, 'Can you drive as far as Bong La?' (which is forty-seven miles, he tells me).
'How many tractors and jeeps do you want? Will you be transporting the porters as well?'
'Six tractors.'
'No, you'll need at least ten.'
'You're only wanting to make money at our expense! Six will be enough.'
'Yes, Sir, no problem.'
They are like children. They enjoy trying to get the better of you. But it's all quite innocent, you mustn't let it upset you.

Every day in Rawalpindi is murder. I can no longer believe PIA when they swear that no flights are possible. By now Sandro and Robert in Skardu must surely have made all the preparations for our approach march.
(Reinhold Messner, diary)

The afternoon is warm and inviting. The wind blows gently across the sandy plains, over the dark boulders and the sun-bleached and sweetly aromatic vegetation. All the green areas are man-made. The Indus in the distance seems quite motionless, a long, curving lake. And the mountains around are like vertical deserts with their huge slopes of scree and their reddish rock, almost violet. On the far side of the river the mountains are higher, topped with snow and ice. The dry wind touches, caresses my skin. The scent of one of the dried herbs that grow here in profusion, wafts up around me. When my foot brushes against one of the clumps, the scent is even more pungent, more pleasant. I pluck a sprig or two as I clamber over a ridge, then I stretch out lazily on a flat, warm rock. Such wilderness calls for meditation, but I can't think of anything to meditate about. So the same few thoughts scamper round and round my head until, finally, I fall asleep.

In the evening a UN-soldier tells us about the border conflict on the Indus. 'Everything is being watched,' he says, 'even the mountains. They shoot at anything. The Gurkhas on the Indian side are not bad chaps, but they are trigger-happy. Theoretically they're supposed to shout "Halt!" and ask who goes there, but usually, they shoot first and ask afterwards.'

The border doesn't follow any logical divide; it is a ceasefire line and takes a completely irrational course. 30,000 soldiers stand on either side of it, keeping a watch on each other. The soldier tells us a couple of stories, 'There was a Pakistani farmer who owned a coconut palm. The Indians claimed that the palm was within their territory. The farmer went across the border every year to gather his fruit, and every year he was given a going-over by the border guards. So after some years it was finally decreed that the tree really did belong in India, but that the farmer would be allowed to harvest the nuts, provided he deliver two baskets of them to the Indians.' And illustrating another aspect of the border dispute, 'The Indians take pot-shots at pigs across the border, whilst the Pakistanis kill cows, which are sacred to the Hindus.'

Robert shakes his head. I am reminded of the Berlin Wall and the machine guns of the 'Vopos'.

20 May
A Dream

There is a lot of water all around us; wild, swirling water fills a swimming pool right to its brim. Wilhelm Bittorf and I find ourselves in the water and he wants to show what he can do. He tries to swim against the strong current. My terror grows with the increasing wildness of the water. I am not sure how it has come about, but we have to rescue my father. It is a hard struggle but finally we manage it. We roll him over so that he can spew out all the water he's swallowed; we force him to vomit. My father is lying unconscious in the corner of the room. I clean the vomit from his lips with a little water. I would not be able to give him artificial respiration with his mouth clogged with sick. My Uncle Ubaldo appears and asks, 'Is there anyone lying on his back?' Then he sees Papa. He approaches him slowly.

21 and 22 May
Truth is what you want it to be

The women, who generally flee and hide whenever we appear – scurrying, rustling, caked in dirt – remind me of the beggarwoman in the deepest

These manners and customs will die out and a new culture and new influences will emerge. The women will no longer go veiled, no longer hide their faces. They will be seen in new hairstyles, no longer wear plaits or curls. With the national awakening, old principles will die, and a new Ka'ba will come into being with western statutes.
(Akbar Allahâbâdi, Urdu poet, nineteenth century)

recess of my soul. The one who torments me constantly and gives me no peace. It is the job of these Balti women to keep the stoves burning and the houses warm for their menfolk; as a consequence of breathing in smoke all day, they grow consumptive. It never occurs to them to question their duty or the superiority of the men. So nothing can change. Will they wake up one day? Perhaps it will be an awakening for all of us when that day comes.

Now they catch sight of me and run away; or, when there are more than two of them together, hide behind their veils, giggling. Having nothing else to do, we airily decide to go the barber's. Village barbers are the same the world over, as are their barber-shops. The only difference here is the absence of girlie calendars. In their place are portraits of lawyer Jinnah, the architect of Pakistan, 'Land of the Pure'. His proud, stern features constrast sharply with the mirrors, the decorative arabesques and the calligraphic designs in an atmosphere otherwise indistinguishable from a Sicilian barber-shop. For five rupees, the owner will give you a scalp massage with his strong, drumming fingers. He offers me a K2 cigarette.

'I don't smoke K2,' I say, 'I go to K2!'

'I smoke K2, you go K2 – Tike?'

The wash-tap is only a foot off the floor. To have my hair washed, I have to kneel down on a wooden board. The water is warm, but it is an unsavoury business, propping oneself up off the slippery floor. Who knows what washings have taken place in this scruffy room before! Meanwhile, the owner is explaining to Robert that his is the finest salon in Skardu. And well it may be; even the PIA booking office makes a pretty grim impression.

While I rub my hair dry with a smelly hand towel, I look out of the door. There are people going up and down, but only men. I spot two monks among them, dressed all in black and walking proudly as their habits befit. They are rather less dust-covered than the others. They meet two other men, embrace, and clasp hands. Such brotherly gestures are quite commonplace here, yet still I find them disturbing.

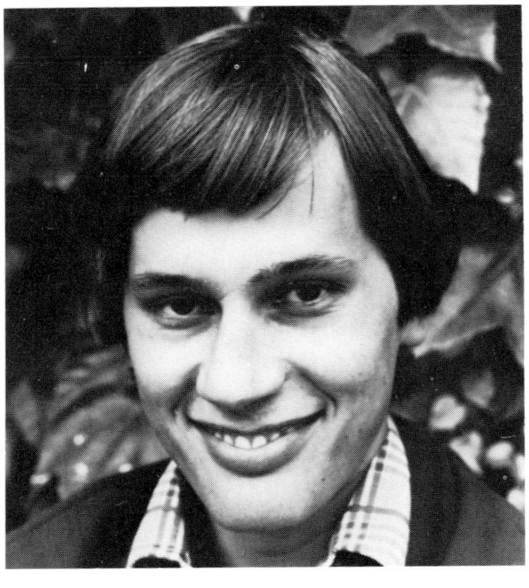

Robert Schauer

We spend the morning beside a little lake where there are some boulders we can scramble about on. But today I am more interested in watching the people, listening to them talking and observing their behaviour. There are gestures and facial expressions which are quite distinct, but which can be interpreted differently by everyone.

Some of the people are smoking, proving to themselves and others how important they are; yet among the poor, smoking really is a vice. One has to accept the customs of the local people. We have grown to accept that a given word has a universal meaning but here we learn that a word is only part of what a person is expressing, only one of the signals he is giving to the person he is addressing. And the truth? That is whatever one wants it to be. But are we any different when we mask with objectivity, what is really only partial and subjective?

23 May

For a week now Robert and I have been waiting in Skardu for the rest of the expedition party. We no longer find ourselves capable of keeping our self-control in the simplest of situations. We even find it hard to smile.

They made us many promises, more than I can remember, but they only kept one of them. They promised to take our land, and they did so.
(Unknown Red Indian)

Sometimes it seems to us that the Pakistanis are deliberately doing their utmost to infuriate us. When they say that a plane is 'standing by' or has 'turned back' or been 'cancelled', it sounds like a litany of excuses, polite but false.
'Tomorrow your friends will be here for sure – inshallah!' If Allah wills. At this point we feel like exploding.
I reply with an ironic, 'Yes, for sure – inshallah!' To no effect because of the suppressed rage behind my caustic retort – that won't do if you really want to cut someone to the quick. But that's me all over. When I ought to show a degree of firmness with petty officials, I am always hindered by awkwardness, and I tend to mask this with bonhomie.
A high-level porter, who has come from the PIA office to offer us his services which we refuse, cannot accept the fact that he has been turned down. He seals the lid on his failure by trotting out the one sentence he knows in English, 'This country is very poor.'
I burst out, 'You want to be poor!' In no way can I excuse or condone my behaviour. I should from the outset have been more positive, tougher, more honest and not allowed compassion to cloud the issue, then the situation would not have arisen. Once again I have come out of it badly; the god-given opportunity has slipped by. Will there be another chance, I wonder? Will there be a time for conciliation?
It is not so much a question of behaving more like a colonial gentlemen than we do; it's being aware of who we are. Up till now I was a colonial gentleman, whilst all the time trying not to be; that is a disastrous contradiction for both sides. I should have been able to refrain perhaps from uttering my final bitter and angry retort about the poverty of this country, had I something more constructive and to the point to replace it. This constant overbalancing of my relationships with other people! I could weep when I think about it.
Again we are waiting in the PIA office for news. When might Reinhold and the others eventually fly in? The office hasn't long been built, but like all recently erected buildings in this area, it appears old.
An air traffic controller is explaining to us in all innocence that of the two aeroplanes we have seen come in from Chitral, one was for parachuting, the other for photographic work. 'For demonstration only.' That's the limit! Here we wait, at no small cost, while they make demonstration flights! Robert curses; 'They have absolutely no sense of reality!' We find their attitude quite incomprehensible in fact.

24 May
First encounter with the Infinite

After the evening meal Robert suggests a walk. Already it's growing progressively darker, but the sky is calm and clear. A few stars have appeared. The high silhouette of Haramosh stands out sharply to the west of us. For a long moment I gaze spellbound at the Pole Star. How nice it is to wander like this: the occasional wisecrack, a view of Skardu, and the wind soft against the face. 'A romantic stroll with neither the moon nor the girl,' I say to myself in my stilted German. We stop near a big tree. Beside its roots an attractive watercourse crosses the street. Its big trunk will shelter us if we sit down. Walking towards it, a dog barks abruptly and a strong wind blows up from nowhere. The foliage of the tree is tossed like storm-lashed waves. At this moment I can actually feel the elements forcing their way into me. Then as I sit down in the lea of the wind, everything becomes quite different. The whole world is reduced to the confines of the lined hood of my anorak, and I try to relate to it. Robert hums away to himself.

25 May
Letter to my Father

. . . I am sure the most important thing you can do is not to think about it. You must try not to let this lurking fear get a grip of you, you mustn't be on the constant lookout for news on the radio or television, or in the papers. The time will pass, inevitably. I want you to know that I think of you, more than you believe. At times like this it can even be a relief when your throat tightens and you have to cry. It's a good feeling in that it brings a son closer to his father, whom for a long time he had lost, so busy was he with his growing up. It is like waking from a bad dream and finding that reality is better, that two people can be close even when they are so far apart they hardly ever write or talk to each other. I hope to drop you a line from Base Camp. Try and think of me as little as possible.
Ciao, with lots of love, A.

26 May
The Baltis and their Roses

The Hotel Baltoro is situated on the southern outskirts of Skardu on the road towards Astor. No signboard proclaims its name. It has no chimney to distinguish it from the other houses. Its only special feature is its pink and yellow painted walls which can be clearly seen, glowing, through the openings in the surrounding wall. The wing of the door is made of plywood, roughly daubed with a white paint. It leads into a dark, roomy hall with comfortable, if musty, sofas and little tables. The rooms themselves are spacious and present a cosy effect, with large, modern, monstrously-patterned, synthetic-fibre carpets. The hotel staff never make the beds; that the guests are expected to do for themselves.

The simple Balti boys often stick a perfumed rose behind their ear. I'm not sure where all the roses come from. Such adornment lends a certain charm to faces and eyes which otherwise might not inspire much trust, displaying rather avidity, brutality and canniness. You seldom see evidence of kindness and goodwill in the Balti face. They look more like birds of prey. But why should we be surprised, our faces are no better. We are no saints.

The hotel cook holds his rose gently between his lips most of the time so that he can enjoy its fine fragrance, an even more bizarre contrast to his coal-black eyes and hawkish appearance. The roses are a living ornament of which I envy the Baltis.

27 May
Arrival in Skardu

It is impossible to find words to describe the confusion, the hustle and excitement of this wonderful day. The other expedition members have arrived, as well as all the baggage. Right away everyone sets about his respective tasks. Robert, Terry and I, accompanied by Hadji Ahmad Khan trot off to the old bazaar. We buy 15 kilos of salt, 50 kilos of butter, 50 kilos of dry milk, 15 kilos of tea, 50 kilos of lentils, half a tonne of meal and 50 kilos of sugar. That is all intended for the porters.

28 May
Dassu

Our departure is enthusiastic and really spectacular. More than a hundred porters, stuffed into a convoy of tractors and jeeps, set off like some latterday Noah's Ark. Halting briefly at Shigar, a village oasis in this desert of stones, we travel on to Bong La, a small town, similarly set in the middle of desert, and 2390 metres above sea level. Now begins the tough hassle with the porters. We have to shout, scold, physically shove them, in order to unite each man with his intended load. They all want a lighter one. Then we have to check that they have each brought their sunglasses and boots which we gave out yesterday.

In Dassu someone tries to steal one of the containers during the night. Ros Ali, our cook boy, spots him at it and chases the thief away. From now on at night we will tie all the loads together with a length of rope.

29 May
People on the Edge

Early in the morning, with Terry's help, I marshall the porters and we set off. I have to run three-quarters of the way to Chakpo to catch up with Reinhold who had gone on ahead. We arrive hours before the others.

In these out-of-the-way villages there are a number of mentally-handicapped people, the result no doubt of long inbreeding. The sight of the local people is depressing. All around there are fields of buckwheat and the women cower down among the plants, hidden by the foliage, but taking care not to tread on the precious crop. The sky is grey and looks very threatening. I am going to have to put on my lined jacket. The wind rustles the apricot trees. That there are people all around is not readily apparent, everywhere seems deserted. Somewhere I hear a child crying but it sounds a long way off. As the first porters arrive, the atmosphere of enchantment vanishes. Noisily they set up the second camp on our long march.

31 May
Askole

Not even the prodigiousness of the peaks can make amends for the equally prodigious ugliness of the valleys.
(Charles Bruce)

Askole is the last habitable refuge in a valley dotted with oases, oases which through centuries of effort, have been wrenched from the desert. You can honestly say that we now find ourselves at the very end of the earth. The extreme poverty, the dirt, the sickness, the intermarriage have all contributed in dragging the people down to a near-animal existence. The houses are of clay and stones with scanty wooden framework; the roofs of mud, topped with thorny bundles of brushwood. Women, with children in their arms, stand outside; animals go in and out through the doors. And over everything, the dust and dirt, fleas and lice.

We notice that the water, which is conducted through irrigation channels, is rationed by the hour, to allow the fields of individual families to be supplied in turn. Wherever there is a lack of water, the grass is very sparse. The few cows, sheep and goats are thin and undersized. During the day they are driven up the hillsides on either side of the Braldo. Often you see yaks perched on walls like chamois.

It is not long before a crocodile of patients queue up, moaning, in front of Ursula, our doctor. There is a woman who has given birth to dead twins and now suffers from pneumonia; a man unable to urinate; people with infections; tuberculosis. I notice that some of us keep our eyes averted. Turning away is the first step towards running away.

The performance is over. I am glad about that. Glad to be done with the

many fleeting emotions. The smell, the language, the paroxyms of coughing, the thick slimy hawking of the sick, the Lambardar who didn't want his wife to have his duvet-jacket (she wasn't with the expedition), these are images that stay with me. In this mood I think, now that could be the last village, the last sad handful of humanity. Can I go on without still being sad thinking of them, not turn back? No good taking it too seriously, we all have to go sooner or later. My only regret would be if I couldn't finish what I'd set out to do.
Sitting on a large boulder in the evening gloom, I become aware how sombre and confused my thoughts are getting.

1, 2, 3 June
Korophon, Barduman and Paiju

To reach the summit one must proceed from encampment to encampment.
(René Daumal, *Mount Analogue*)

For two long days we waited under a bleak and miserable sky. But overnight the wild scudding greyness, in which from time to time flocks of silent crows were tossed, dissolved away. The weather is now beautiful. Even the thick, sluggish Braldo has been transformed into a lively, spring torrent. Fine sand and pollen drifts over the tents. (Reinhold Messner)

We recruit twelve more porters in Askole for the march-in, eleven to carry 300 kilos of meal, another for the sugar. That brings us up to 148 Balti porters. That's nothing exceptional, there have been bigger expeditions.
It seems to be developing into a bad day. The sky is hopelessly grey. Ursula, jumping from one rock to another, loses her balance and injures her right ankle. It looks serious; a torn ligament, an open wound, shock. Robert administers first aid. We all stand round.
We are unable to make radio contact with Skardu. Who knows when we could order a helicopter? But Ursula has to be got back whatever. Reinhold and Friedl take it in turns to carry her back to Askole on their shoulders. The rest of us carry on.
I am so upset by the accident, I cannot find words to describe it. I think of Ursula returning to Germany, to a clinic. Her share of the adventure is well and truly over, and with it a part of our expectations too.
The morning of 3 June is fine and for the first time K2 looms up at the end of the valley. It gradually comes into view behind the Biale Tower. The summit wears a bonnet of cloud, shaped like a gigantic lens. This perfect white brushstroke in the blue sky stirs my imagination.

4 June

The fact that one becomes what one is, presupposes that one has not the remotest suspicion of what one is.
(Friedrich Nietzsche, *Ecce Homo*)

Stumbling and slipping, I drag myself up and down the undulations of the Baltoro Glacier, staggering, swearing. Finally the narrow track across the scree approaches a broad, comfortable plateau – Liligo. All morning the Trango Towers were the dumb witnesses of my tedious pilgrimage. I feel weak. Looking back, I see the long Braldo Valley, our link back to the outside world, and the endless column of porters. They are the lucky ones, they can go back.
At 17.00 hours Reinhold and Friedl return. Their forced march from Skardu doesn't seem to have affected them at all. They reached Askole with Ursula on 1 June, but had to wait two days for a helicopter from Gilgit.
During the night the songs and dances of the Baltis keep us awake. I lie there contemplating my various irksome complaints: stabbing pains in my liver, catarrh, backache. Renato, who is sharing the tent with me, has fleas. These discomforts and disorders are now my chief preoccupation, day in, day out. I am suddenly struck with the suspicion that they may all be traced back to the fact that I feel a sense of inferiority compared to the others. Are they really stronger than I? To feel like this, imagining the

others endowed with more strength, competence, endurance and other such manly virtues, is like a cancer in my make-up. I cannot eradicate it.

5 June
Freedom of the Mountain Goats

Already the sun is bathing the great granite towers in a rosy glow; they cast enormous shadows. The Baltoro Glacier seems to wake and stretch itself in the warmth of the early morning. The porters make their preparations for departure with greater care than usual. They know they can expect nothing but rough stones and ice all day long. 133 men – we have already dismissed 15 – call to Allah, asking him to stand by them on their journey up the glacier. Their singing seems to fill the hollow of the valley, the sound to reach the sky. For a long moment I, with them, experience communion with God.
In the dazzle off the Baltoro, I say to myself; 'This is one of those rare, precious moments, to have once had the opportunity to see this primeval landscape.' I am happy, I run and dance on the glacier, then pause to select the memories I want to keep from among the unending possibilities. Early this morning I spotted a herd of mountain goats. Now I feel as if something of their freedom has brushed off on me.

6 June
The Difficulties of Communal Living

Our goal today is an ill-defined spot on the glacier called Horo. We reach it at 14.00 hours. A hefty wind greets us. The total impression is one of chaos and wildness. Freezing, we huddle amongst the rocks to await the porters.
An outburst of anger erupts during the meal, which we don't bother to suppress. It proves our relationship is moving into a less formal, more honest level. Let's hope we keep it that way. On any expedition, each new day brings incidents that highlight the difficulties of living together. Sadly, not everyone knows how hard it is to get along amicably – quite apart from any language barrier.

7 and 8 June
A Lot of Patience is required

Leaving Horo, Robert has convinced me that there is nothing wrong with my liver. He says it's my diaphragm. We wade on through quite deep snow.
Porters carrying loads of 30 kilos catch up with me and overtake. I feel very ashamed of myself. In the evening we reach the immense amphitheatre where the Baltoro and Godwin-Austen Glaciers join.
I am worn out from ploughing through the knee-deep snow all day and my feet are soaked through. It's all I needed! I can just muster enough energy to whistle for a meal and a box to sit on, then I fling myself into my tent to get some sleep. There is always something, it seems, to dishearten me. And of course I do make things difficult for myself. I always want to be everywhere at once, I worry that the shovel will get lost in the snow, that the cook won't seal up the damaged mustard tubes properly, that they're using too much fuel, or too much sugar. I worry in case the weather should take a turn for the worse, that the porters won't be able to cross the difficult glacier ahead. And more than anything I worry about my health, I lie in wait for every trivial twinge.

Ursula Grether

9 June
Death and Guilt

Hard and difficult is the journey to death, and fearful the way. The goal is a long way off, the burdens heavy on our shoulders. Make ready for the journey, don't blindly delay, don't hang your heart on your transitory home.
(Osman Ihsani, Urdu poet, seventeenth century)

Some nights later Renato is to write about today, saying 'Something happened that has touched me deeply.' Today, 9 June, is the day one of our porters, Ali, son of Kazim of Askole, is killed. A man getting killed touches everyone, but especially those who have never been on a big expedition before.
Already in the half-light of early morning our cramped encampment on the ice resembles a swarming anthill. The 125 Baltis are up and about earlier than usual so that they can climb the glacier whilst the surface of the snow is still hard. Their clearing of throats and coughing, as they slowly warm up after a night in the open at 5000 metres, echos like a rebuke. Small, scattered fires are burning round about. Wood – brought up from Paiju – is being chopped to make tea and warm unleavened bread. Terry has to shout in an attempt to check their impatience. Reinhold and Friedl set off ahead to break trail. Then the others, strongest first, are allowed to follow. Michl and I are in the middle. Through one narrow, icy gully Reinhold fixes a rope. Above, the wall of seracs gleam. We are approaching the slopes of the Angelus, in order to climb up around to the west and into the Savoia Basin.
Reinhold discovers an exposed, but easy, way through the snow-covered band of rock and fixes a rope on it. Fearfully the first porters attempt it, the others shake their heads. The traverse ends on a terrace where the glacier no longer poses any threat. Beyond the rocks, we will be able to continue without difficulty. Some specially courageous porters swing back and forth, carrying up loads for the weaker ones, who then follow. They attach themselves to the fixed ropes, trembling and praying.
Michl and I also help shift loads. Suddenly I am startled by shrieks. Further up, on the easier terrain, one of the porters has fallen into a crevasse. Not heeding the warnings of Terry and Reinhold, the man had left the safe spot on the glacier and suddenly broken through into a hidden hollow. Reinhold, Terry and I immediately lower Friedl down into the crevasse on a rope, but he finds the man dead. The body is fifteen metres down, jammed between two ice walls which meet like the neck of a funnel. Later we lower Robert down; he, too, is unable to free the porter. So the place of his death becomes also his grave.
There follows some confusion. The porters don't want to go any further. Reinhold, who had run on ahead to the proposed site for Base Camp, comes back. He reports that the traverse to the Negrotto Saddle is

Panorama showing the Baltoro, Abruzzi and Godwin-Austen Glaciers; far left, K2.

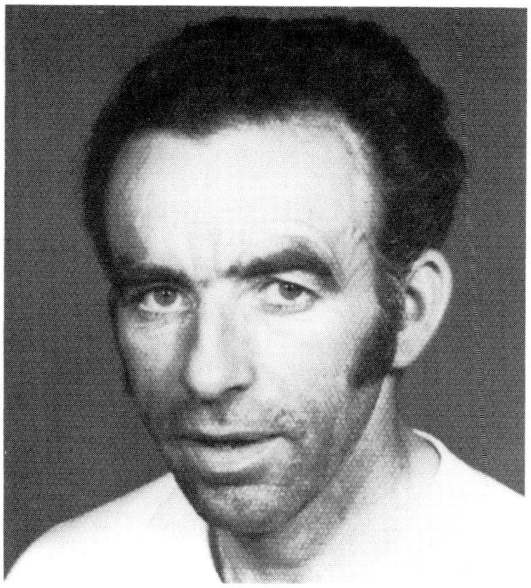

Michl Dacher

We are six individuals, each responsible for himself.
(Reinhold Messner)

threatened by a precarious icefall. Nor would it be possible for the porters to make it there in a single day. So, retreat. Reinhold makes a quick decision. We will put our camp on the traditional Italian Base Camp site. The porters' faces are etched with tiredness from the exhausting march and the death of their comrade. Wearily, they permit themselves to be led down the mountain, many on their bottoms. Their heavy loads threaten to overtopple them.

Between K2 and Broad Peak the heat smoulders. The ice is matt, and lustreless. Chogolisa and the Mitre can be seen rising in the distance. We shall be staying on this fermenting ice for two long months. I can hardly wait for this expedition to end!

In the evening Terry remarks that it is God's will that we have to set up our camp here and not where we planned. 'Ali had to die today,' he says, 'he had to come all this long way in order to die here.'

Nevertheless, I sense that we all feel guilty even if we don't show it. I am of the opinion that it is better to accept the guilt. If you set off on an expedition, you ought to know what could be in store. Certainly the porters are frightened of dying, but they take it in their stride. Their harsh lives give them no cause for illusions. Anyone who is too deeply influenced by the death of his comrade, is really displaying fear at the prospect of his own end. And that is the guilt, the true guilt.

12 June
Relaxing with Fists Clenched

Renato, my tent mate, now has a special role to play in this great game in which we are all, at one and the same time, pawns, bishops, kings and queens. It is with Renato that I talk the most. When I discuss things with Reinhold, I am aware that a barrier exists between us, which we would probably both like to overcome. Even with Renato, it sometimes becomes tiresome, difficult. I don't want to run the risk of talking too much – after all, he needs his peace too, time to be alone with his thoughts.

One evening I confide in him that I have a suspicion that Reinhold no longer intends to attempt his 'Magic Line'. He seems to be tending towards a quicker, alpine solution instead. Renato immediately rolls over towards me in his sleeping bag. Eyes wide, like someone who has been given the opportunity to reveal a secret, he says, 'I've noticed that too.' And immediately a strange feeling rushes through me. Like clenching and unclenching of fists. In a surge of affection, I say to Renato that we ought always to be honest with each other.

'You must speak up,' I say, 'one of us alone may not be enough, it needs both of us.'
I feel very close to him.
Tomorrow we are to reconnoitre the first 1200 metres of the Abruzzi Spur, but I can't say I relish the prospect. My rucksack is ready, but I'm not.

16 June
With Renato on the Abruzzi Spur

Tanzan and Ekido were once travelling together down a muddy road. A heavy rain was still falling. Coming around a bend, they met a lovely girl in a silk kimono and sash, unable to cross the intersection. 'Come on girl,' said Tanzan at once, lifting her in his arms, he carried her over the mud. Ekido did not speak again until that night when they reached a lodging temple. Then he could no longer restrain himself. 'We monks don't go near females,' he told Tanzan, 'especially not young and lovely ones. It is dangerous. Why did you do that?' 'I left the girl there,' said Tanzan, 'are you still carrying her?
(Zen story, related in Base Camp)

We make an early start from Base Camp. Robert and Michl set off on skis in the direction of the British Base Camp, from where we had originally envisaged launching our attempt on the 'Magic Line'. Friedl and Reinhold go off to the South Face of K2 hoping to push up at least as far as the 'Nose', the steep serac bluff which bars the way to the huge and dangerous cliffs higher up. Renato and I are to start a reconnaissance in the direction of the Abruzzi Spur.
A wide moraine ridge, sloping on both sides, leads up from Base Camp – Renato dubs it 'The Autobahn'. It is flanked by two glacier streams which separate it from the two main ice arms of the Godwin-Austen Glacier. Initially the way to the Spur seems level. Only when we reach the big step in the glacier does it become difficult to locate a way through the crevasses and overhanging pillars of rock. The Abruzzi Spur, a conspicuous, sharply-detailed rib of rock which seems to tower above us indefinitely, is a good 2000 metres high.
Slowly we climb up to the right of the pillar. We are beginning to feel the effects of the altitude. I have difficulty in drawing breath, and Renato is not much better. As we rest, foreheads pressed to ice-axes, struggling for air, it occurs to us that we have taken on too much, and that it would be better to call a halt at 5700 metres. There is nowhere where we could put an intermediate camp.
At 14.00 hours I finally spot the place where earlier expeditions have camped. We are now at 6100 metres, 1100 metres above Base Camp. The tent is small, the air thin. With a deal of contortion, Renato and I succeed in thawing some snow. Elbows propped on two mats, I endeavour to collect chunks of snow from outside the door of the tent. There is no time for thinking. We concentrate solely on drinking the soup, and later orange juice. After the second mug of juice and the second helping of soup, I worry that our butane/propane gas cylinder won't last out for heating our camomile tea tonight and our breakfast in the morning.

18 June
What counts?

Yesterday we climbed back down to Base Camp. We all sit down to breakfast together. Renato declares he has no interest in the Abruzzi Spur. He finds it very hard to abandon our original plan and enthuse over a compromise. Slowly the discussion switches to the theme whether, in our case, it would make more sense to climb to the summit, or tackle the difficult pillar of our planned line. Reinhold thinks it would be better to launch an attempt on the summit, even though the route is not particularly difficult. He acknowledges that a couple of years ago he often made fun of summit aspirations, but meanwhile he has come to appreciate that the summit is the place where all knots untie themselves, the place without which no mountain is conceivable.
'K2 is a "Magic Mountain" and even the known route has its own magic,'

Renato Casarotto

he says.
Friedl is not up to much, he has a fever. All the same he affirms that it was the summit that induced him to come along.
At this precise moment a huge piece breaks off from one of the seracs, right between the Abruzzi Spur and the South-East Rib, which we had discussed as a possibility for an alpine-style ascent. Had one of us been on it now, he would certainly not have come away alive. The answer to that particular question is clear – to me at any rate – nothing will induce me to set foot on that narrow ridge.
Reinhold says he feels sure, though he couldn't prove it for certain, that his 'Magic Line' wouldn't now be possible, what with the accidents, nor justifiable. 'We are too few; Ursula's gone; the Base Camp is here and not there, and we have only got six weeks.' Robert and Michl are also in favour of a swift attack on the summit.
Finally it's my turn. Do I consider the summit of K2 to be more important than the aesthetic perfection of the line? I answer, 'In my opinion the summit is not important, not even on K2. But equally, it's unimportant to risk your life on a difficult face. Given the choice and knowing that I could not make the hard face, I would go off and climb a different mountain altogether. That way the summit would remain. Whilst it's true, as I say, that the summit is not important in itself, it is nevertheless a point where I find I can give expression to my inner energy. If my energy can find expression and fulfilment up there, it comes back to me changed. That is the real reason why I climb.'

The only way of safeguarding our chances of the summit. (Robert Schauer)

We finally agree to attempt the Abruzzi Rib, even though others have climbed it before us.

20 June

Yesterday was a bad day for me. I was in such a sorry state, physically and emotionally exhausted, that I thought I should never manage to climb K2 and that it was quite pointless for me to have come. And I still feel the same today. I don't want to spell out my troubles, sufficient to reaffirm my discontent. I feel like a motherless child, abandoned and lonely in this tent – which, incidentally, I would prefer to have all to myself. Renato is no help to me at all. Nor could he be. They're all well, the others, nothing the matter with them. But whenever I look at myself, all I see is this pathetic, wobbling, wheezing creature. When will it all end? When will this accursed expedition finally come to an end, so that I don't continually have to be faced with these people?

Baltoro, Karakorum

The Great Himalayan Range consists in reality of a series of ranges together forming a great arc whose outer side faces due south. To the north lies the boundless table-land of Tibet, to the south the depression of the Indus and the Ganges. At its two extremities the series of ranges falls away and curves southwards, forming in the east the mountains of Burma, in the west the hills of Baluchistan. On this side, however, almost adjoining the northern extremity of the Himalaya proper, is an enormous corrugation in the earth's surface containing a chain of exceedingly high mountains, commonly called the Karakorum, after its best-known and most important pass, the Karakorum Pass. The word karakorum *signifies in Tibetan 'black'* (kara) *'gravel or earth covered with detritus'* (korum)*; and from its initial letter are derived the abbreviations K1, K2, K3 etc., which have been adopted by the Indian Topographical Office as a means of identifying a very numerous series of peaks without local names.*
(Ardito Desio)

Mount Everest (8848 m) might be loftier than K2 (8611 m); the enormous bulk of Kangchenjunga (8579 m) might appear more menacing; but the totally unrealised wealth of its beauty, the diversity and nobility of its summits, the overwhelming richness of its mountaineering potential . . . makes the Baltoro region truly unique. It is the ideal area, not only for the active mountaineer, but indeed for anyone responsive to alpine beauty.
(Günther Oskar Dyhrenfurth)

In outline it resembles the Matterhorn, yet it would take no less than forty-one Matterhorns to assemble the amount of rock from which K2 is constructed.
(Wilhelm Bittorf)

Right: The pyramid of K2, seen from the south-west. The 'Magic Line' was to have run from the notch in the bottom left of the picture, up the spur onto the level icefield (the Mushroom) in the centre, then continue, bearing right, up the Sickle and the Gully to the South Summit, from where it would continue without difficulty to the Main Summit.
The West Ridge is seen in profile (left). This was attempted unsuccessfully by a British expedition in 1978 under the leadership of Chris Bonington. Between these two ridges, in shadow, lies the West Face. Right of the South Ridge, half sunlit, half in shade, is the mighty South Face of K2. Friedl Mutschlechner and Reinhold Messner, reconnoitring this face, succeeded in getting as far as the lower edge of the barrier of ice cliffs which block the central right hand section of the face.

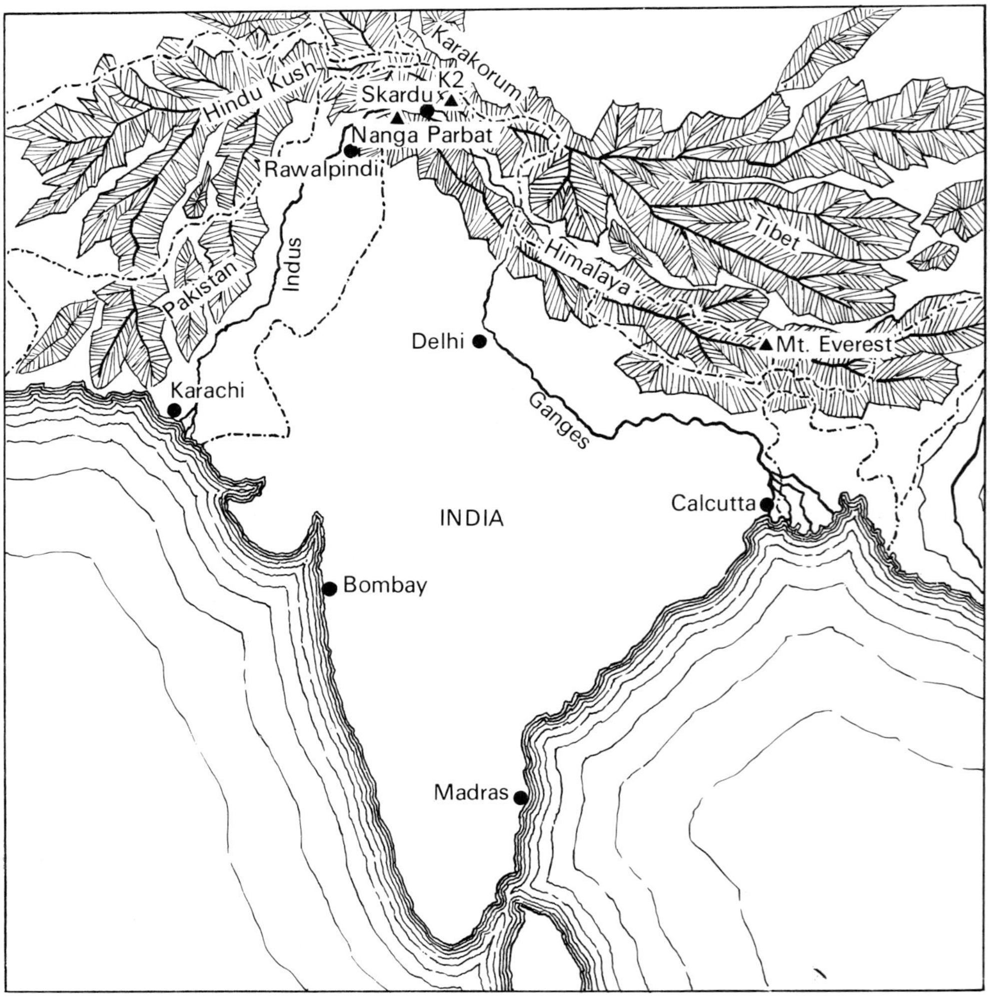

Politically, the Karakorum constitutes a frontier between territories administered on the one hand by Russia and China, on the other by India and Pakistan.
(Ardito Desio)

It is not K2 the mountain alone that beckons it is the country, it is these people.
(Reinhold Messner)

Rawalpindi, close to the modern metropolis of Islamabad, remains the unofficial capital of Pakistan. It hardly seems to have an oriental air but rather the character of a Wild West town – only the cowboys are missing.

K2 is not just the name of a mountain, it is the trademark too of the most smoked cigarette in Pakistan. The kiosks also sell lemonade and papers – but no German newspapers of course.

Next double page: The Messner expedition has to wait more than ten days in Rawalpindi for the flight to Skardu, capital of Baltistan. In Skardu they hire 136 porters and then the long march to K2 begins.

The air above Rawalpindi and Skardu rises during the course of the day, and the smoke hanging above the mud-houses – in the mornings still white and patchy – gradually fades away into the nebulous mass above. (Reinhold Messner)

Skardu: smoky, dusty, dirty. Cultural monuments are a rarity.

Centuries have gone by since Buddhism was the religion of the Baltis; they were forcibly converted to Islam. Just occasionally you can still find ancient cult relics. The villages make a wretched impression. The only thing that softens the image are the age-old poplars and apricot trees.
(Renato Casarotto)

The Baltis live in simple two-storey houses constructed of mud, stones and wood, yet they are completely self-sufficient. In Askole expeditions have traditionally hired porters and purchased food for them: *atta* (meal) and *ghee* (butterfat).

The journey from Dassu to Askole is a long trudge up the wild valley of the Braldo. In some places the path ahead disappears from view, in others it emerges into the open. Sometimes it leads up the face of the mountain, sometimes it winds its way among the rocks at the edge of the river. (Ardito Desio)

In Askole – where roads have no names, houses no numbers and people are unregistered at birth – I, too, gradually shed my numerate existence. (Reinhold Messner)

In place of authority, a respect for one another. (Alessandro Gogna)

Wherever tributaries run down from the steep barren hillsides and disgorge into the Braldo, the Baltis have created tiny habitable oases with a complicated irrigation system. The fields are stacked one above the other in terraces, and guarantee a living for a few dozen families at a time. Even so, fodder and wood have to be brought in from further afield.

Next double page: During the winter months, young and old alike retreat into their huts.

For these people, who from birth are inured to the hardest of exertions, and who are used to carrying everything they need for survival on their backs, it is not unusual to carry loads of 20 or 30 kilos. Most are illiterate. They are encrusted with dirt. Far from civilisation no-one has taught them to wash themselves regularly, or even to read. To them it is perfectly natural to live like this. It doesn't take much to make them happy: a cigarette, a sweet, a friendly gesture, a greeting. Immediately a radiant smile breaks across their whole face.
(Renato Casarotto)

The inhabitants of the main valleys of the Karakorum belong to at least six different races. Reading from west to east, these are the Brokpa, the Baltis, the Purighi, the Dardi, the Ladaki and the Changpa. The most numerous ethnical groups are represented by the Baltis and the Ladaki; the Baltis inhabiting valleys of the western Karakorum, the Ladaki the eastern valleys. As regards religion, the Baltis are for the most part Muslim while the Ladaki are followers of Buddha. The languages of these peoples all belong to the Tibetan family: Urdu and Hindustani are the linguae francae *of the region.*
(Ardito Desio)

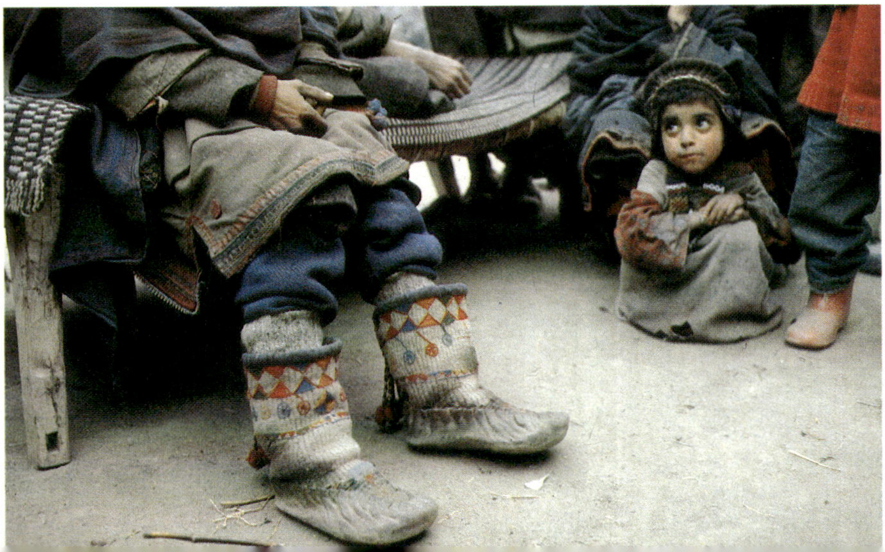

In the mountains of Baltistan there is no form of medical care at all. The people do not grow to be old, and the child mortality rate is high.

Up there we live without hurry or compulsion; sometimes without giving any thought to yesterday or tomorrow. It seems to me that this is the way to achieve personal equilibrium. (Reinhold Messner)

1

2

7

3

4

5

6

The granite walls towering above the Baltoro Glacier are impressive: 1: The Cathedral; 2: Biaho Tower; 3: Fore-summit of Paiju Peak; 4: Lesser and Greater Trango Towers; 5: Cathedral and Lobsang; 6: Cave at the mouth of the Baltoro Glacier (seen from Paiju); 7: Panorama between Paiju Peak and Cathedral.

The wilderness not only encircles us; this prehistoric landscape also prevails within campsites and along the route, which unfolds as we go along.
(Reinhold Messner)

Left: View from Baltoro Glacier towards Paiju Peak (6599 m, the prominent peak on the left) and Uli Biaho Tower.

My legs began to grow stronger and steadier crossing this rough terrain. Without doubt scrambing over the undulations and between the rocks developed strength and balance. (Reinhold Messner)

Shaped like a roof, Chogolisa (7654 m) in evening light. It was from the left hand ridge (in shadow) that Hermann Buhl fell to his death in 1957 when a cornice collapsed.

The *preceding double page:* Shows the Trango Towers (left) and Paiju Peak (right) in early morning light. These smoothly-polished granite walls are more than 2000 metres high.

The sun goes down – far away over the jagged horizon. Just as if there were nothing behind it. (Reinhold Messner)

The Braldo River squeezes its way through a wall of rock.

So long as I look for easy practical explanations, then I can see no sense in our undertaking. Sensibleness plays no part in my adventuring. Whatever I do, wherever I

go or climb, the question of sense melts away.
(Reinhold Messner)

The heat of the sun continuously frets away at the glaciers.

Though Gasherbrum IV is not one of the 8000 metre peaks, it is one of the most beautiful mountains in the world. It was first climbed in 1958 by Walter Bonatti and Carlo Mauri. The steep West Face, however, in the centre of the picture presents a fascinating alpine problem. It has often been attempted, but so far without success. Crumbling rock, stone and icefalls add to its difficulties.

Ahead of us, there it stands, this summit pyramid. It all makes absolute sense without being at all rational or irrational.
(Reinhold Messner)

1

2

3

The eight-thousanders of the Karakorum and the celebrated Mustagh Tower, a seven-thousander: (1) Mustagh Tower 7263 m; (2) Gasherbrum IV 7980 m; III 7925 m and II 8035 m; (3) Gasherbrum I (Hidden Peak) 8068 m; (4) K2 8611 m; (5) Broad Peak 8047 m. All these mountains have been climbed.

4

5

These summits! They make a sensual impact on me, produce a feeling that courses through my body, rather than a sequence of thoughts in my head. (Reinhold Messner)
These giants ought one day to be tackled like the great faces of the Alps. The smaller the team, the bigger the challenge. (Chris Bonington)

Left: To date only one route has been traced on Masherbrum (7820 m), not on the precipitous North-East Face, shown here, but on the southern side.
Below: Four eight-thousanders huddle together in one small area of the Karakorum: K2, Broad Peak, Gasherbrum II and I (Hidden Peak). There are also a number of high seven-thousanders and the incomparably beautiful granite towers which fringe the Baltoro Glacier. For years the Karakorum was closed to foreign expeditions for political reasons, but since 1975, year by year ever more expedition teams have been active in this wild mountain region. The approach is via Rawalpindi and Skardu (air links possible this far), and then up the Braldo Gorge and the Baltoro Glacier.

As their angular unweathered forms show, these mountains are geologically of recent age, being as young as the Cretaceous period and perhaps even as the Tertiary. At about the centre of the range K2 rises to over 8500 metres. (Tom Longstaff)

The most formidable obstacle to overcome on the journey from Rawalpindi to Skardu is a deep valley carved by the Indus between the Nanga Parbat group (8125 m) and the Haramosh group (7397 m). There is no possibility of avoiding this valley, which is, moreover, frequently obscured by clouds. And since the flight is effected by an aircraft which when loaded has not a sufficiently high ceiling to cross the mountains in question, good visibility is essential so that the pilot can follow the tortuous corridor which separates them. (Ardito Desio)

The sun first catches the summits of Paiju Peak and Masherbrum like an enormous rosy spotlight. Then it lights up a snow summit behind the blunt, skyscraper-steep Trango Towers, throwing them into sharp outline. Next, the Trangos themselves come alive: smooth walls, fluted walls, slender towers, ponderous domes, rough-hewn corners . . . a brutal sculpture in bronze granite. Beside them in total contrast sits the finely-detailed, subtly-graduated pyramid of the Grand Cathedral and separated by a 2000 metre cleft. Above these seven-thousanders rises the summit of K2. (Wilhelm Bittorf)

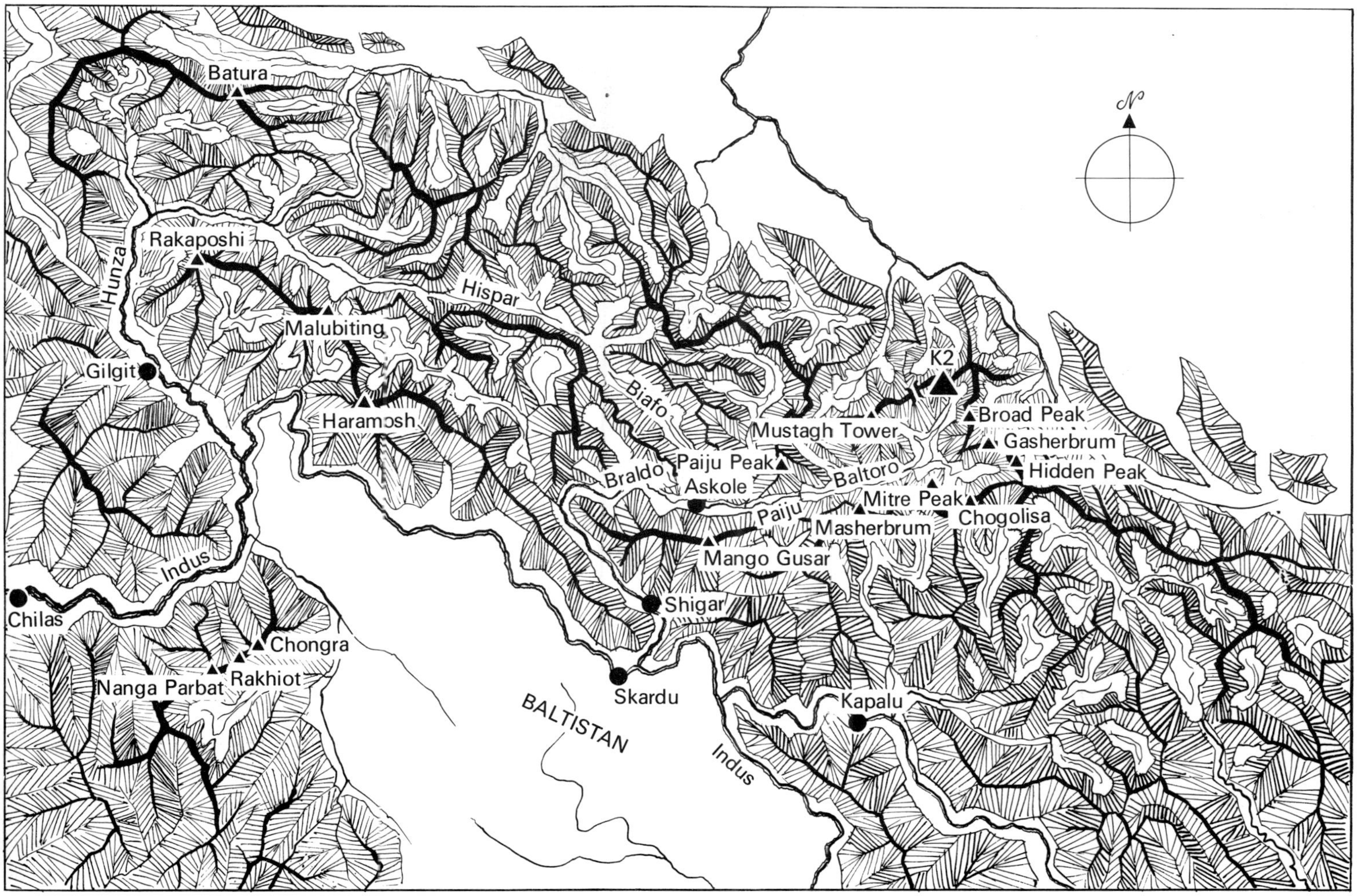

The Other Face of K2

Ros Alí is just bringing the tea into the tent. I think about home, about everything I have left behind. It's true I chose to come here, wanted the larger scale of things, yet I can't seem to handle it, feeling isolated as I do. My strength comes and goes, and I suffer like a dog. I find it difficult to lower the defences of this fortress in which I have imprisoned myself. I'm talking about lethargy, and the ballast from so many years of education, and the dictum of commonsense.

21 June
Summer Solstice

I want to know whether I decided to come on this prospective adventure out of personal conceit, or whether it is the desire towards self-knowledge and self-realization that once again drives me on. (Alessandro Gogna)

This damned inactivity! All you can say for it is that it does sometimes call for the interchange of feelings and ideas.
Michl is pleasant and unassuming. I enjoy his company and he appreciates my friendly overtures. We understand each other only with difficulty. He knows little Italian, and we communicate more by intuition than with words.
Reinhold is stretched out on the ground like a cat enjoying the sun. I get ready to leave for one of the high camps. My rucksack is not heavy. It doesn't seem right to be setting off with such an unimportant load.
'What are you making so much fuss about,' says Reinhold. 'Just go. It really doesn't matter.'
I try to protest again, but my insistence irritates him.
'I don't want to go now, you've put me off,' I snap, and toss off the rucksack. So, I don't leave today, and there's a lump in my throat.
After the evening meal, a more relaxed and homely atmosphere prevails. Someone suggests coffee. Spontaneously we all start talking to each other. For a change we speak in Italian. The conversation keeps coming back to the same theme: the climber in search of his identity.
'Identity is a privilege for whoever has it. You don't get it by envying someone else's,' I begin.
'When I was young I was only able to go to the Dolomites once a year, climbing. There I used to see people like Bonatti, Brandler, Desmaison. By that time they were already able to travel, make expensive journeys. But I didn't go around saying they had behaved immorally, or had sold themselves. At most I felt a healthy envy at their activities, and that is something quite different.'
It is mostly Reinhold and I, along with Joachim and Renato, who get steamed up on this subject.
Joachim: 'There are no real sponsors when it comes to climbing. Any financial gain can only be made after any enterprise.'
'It's my opinion that certain people criticise the concept of free expeditions so emphatically for the simple reason that they know it will be fuel to the fire for hundreds of envious gossip-mongers.'
Reinhold: 'After all that's the way climbing started, with a reward offered to Balmat for the ascent of Mont Blanc.'
I get great satisfaction out of the fact that we understand each other so well, and that Joachim and Reinhold are speaking Italian for our benefit.
Reinhold: 'It's our own fault if alpinism has no identity, or to be more exact, if some climbers don't possess it. The mass media make a bomb out of it. They project a completely absurd and false picture of mountaineering, and we do absolutely nothing to alter this position. Indeed sometimes we even believe in it ourselves.'

Reinhold Messner belonged in the front rank of those young climbers who rebelled against the old military way of organising things, the cult of comradeship and heroism; and who in the new spirit of the times blew the wind of change into mountaineering. (Wilhelm Bittorf)

K2 from the south-east.

'Like sheep,' I say, 'if you kill the wolf, then everyone is on your side. If you defend the wolf, the enemy, then that too is accepted, for basically the flock is not unwilling to live in fear and be torn to pieces. But if you dare encroach upon the shepherd, the sheepdog, if you take on the established order, the overwhelming traditions, because you and your group want to see clearly, free from the burden of taboos and outmoded ideas, then you run the danger of being pounced on, and thousands of clopping hooves will trample you underfoot. That is the "Flight from Freedom" your Erich Fromm talks about, the "Liberté pour quoi faire".'
Joachim: 'You're right. They're frightened at the prospect of freedom.'
'Like that time in Innsbruck,' recalls Reinhold, 'at a congress of the Swiss, German and Austrian alpine clubs. I had only been speaking for seven minutes before I had the impression I had fallen among savages. Respectable people of 50, 60, 70 years old, jumped out of their chairs, shaking their fists, their hair wild and their eyes bloodshot! I had only said that in my opinion the practical activities of alpine clubs ought to be curtailed; not so many way-markings on tracks, no over-abundance of literature on individual climbs and routes – short instructions would be sufficient. Otherwise there would be a danger – I didn't say it was inevitable – that the member of an alpine club would experience some kind of travel-agency-adventure in the mountains, "all inclusive", with the result that every real adventure would be killed from the start. Hardly had I uttered the words "Experience-insurance," than all hell broke loose. I had to give up.'
Meanwhile, outside, Chogolisa – 'Bride Peak' – had taken on a very delicate, velvety pink. It is at moments like this when I am overawed with the beauty of creation.
After three strenuous days with very little to show for it, I am quite pessimistic. Six of us climbed up together the day before yesterday: Reinhold, Michl, Renato, me, and the two porters, Ros Alí and Gulam Mahdi.

22 June

Messner and Dacher climb from Base Camp (4950 m) to Camp I (6100 m). Gogna and Casarotto follow up the same day, the two parties erecting two two-man tents.
(Joachim Hoelzgen)

At 3.30 we gather for breakfast. The rucksacks are packed. I am not ready in time. The others are soon far ahead. I seem to be always at the tail-end. Will I always be the one hobbling behind?
Where the glacier rises steeply, we cross a huge plateau. Avalanches pose a constant threat here. I have often seen how the lethal waves have swept right across to the face of Broad Peak opposite.
The climb up to Camp I is murder. I realise there's always something that prevents me from feeling perfectly well. Either I'm weak from diarrhoea or find it difficult to breathe through my nose. At times like this I am happier on my own. Then I don't have to compare my dragging progress with the others. It makes me really wretched, seeing them move easily and not needing as many rests.
How curious this wretchedness is! Here we are amongst incomparable surroundings, six men venturing to climb an eight-thousander – and I feel wretched. And this wretchedness is paradoxical, too. My petty ego still wants to be in the centre of things; everything must relate solely to it. So the hours drag slowly by.
It is hard work fashioning a platform in the ice and clearing the scree on

Concealed in the heart of all beings is the Atman, the spirit, the self; though invisible, it can be seen by the seers of the subtle, when their vision is pure and clear. (Kath Upanishad)

either side. But it seems easier than the last time.
Darkness falls. I am somewhat rested. Now it is time for some camomile tea. Cooking has become a ritual. As there are no Sherpas here to bring us drinks into the tent, we have to do it all ourselves. Today, for the first time, Michl and Reinhold are sharing a tent. I hear them talking animatedly. Then it gradually grows quiet.

23 June

Messner and Dacher climb House's Chimney and up to Camp II (6700 m), which corresponds to Camp V of earlier expeditions and still contains pathetic remnants of six Japanese tents. Gogna and Casarotto follow them up bringing two lengths of rope, and then climb back down to spend the night in Camp I.
(Joachim Hoelzgen)

This next day is hard. Reinhold and Michl want to fix ropes, set up Camp II and spend the night there. Renato and I are to follow them up with tents, ropes and radio apparatus. Once passed a rock spur, made easier by having a metal ladder in place, we come upon the platform for what was the fourth camp of the earlier Italian expedition. We permit ourselves a short rest, but wait a long time for Renato. It is cold and over the ridge, a stronger wind is blowing. House's Chimney, which is the biggest obstacle below Camp II, leads straight up from here to the edge of a yellow spur. Above it the storm howls. The ice at the foot of the chimney lies like a white damask napkin. Where it clings to the rock fissure, it has an angle of 60 degrees. Once above it, we see a handful of red tents, torn to shreds by the wind and two muffled, hunched figures, their faces encrusted with ice. Reinhold and Michl settle themselves in here for the night. The storm is now so violent that we can no longer understand each other, even when we bellow. As Renato arrives, I feel tempted to descend right away, but first of all I secure the last rope. It is a situation like many I have been in before, a dramatic retreat, secured to a line which, like our hands, is very weak. We are attached to karabiner and rope, so that we can never slip very far, only down to our next anchorage.
The storm is less fierce down in Camp I.
After the third night in Camp I, I feel better. Renato, though, is feeling weak. He wants neither the breakfast I have prepared, nor to get dressed. We have to get further down; the storm outside is still bad.
The glacier in the meantime has changed considerably. It is now only partly covered in snow and this continually breaks under our weight. Sometimes there's water underneath, so that we sink in up to our middles. We reach Base Camp at 12 o'clock, where Robert and the others welcome us warmly.

26 June
A Find in the Snow

The sun has gone down behind the rocks of the Angelus and the air grows cold. The scant snow still lying around Base Camp grows crisp. Reinhold and Joachim are talking in their tent, Renato dozes, Terry, Friedl and I watch Robert skiing. Suddenly one of his ski-tips hits something metallic. Robert digs and unearths a yellow oxygen cylinder. After the first surprise, he has another go, and one by one, pulls out 20 cylinders. 'I'm a rich man,' he shouts jubilantly. It must be the surplus oxygen from the Whittaker expedition. To us it is worthless. We have all resolved not to use any oxygen at all on K2.

28 June
The Voice of the Wind

Robert and Friedl have been away for 24 hours. At 4.20 Renato and I leave the mess tent where Ros Alí has been making us tea. We move slowly, crossing the glacier. I draw level with Renato. On the summit of K2 a cloud banner is streaming like a plume of frozen mist; it glows in the

In a storm rising to hurricane force, Schauer and Mutschlechner climb up to Camp II with two tents. Gogna and Casarotto move to Camp I and just manage to prevent one of the tents there from blowing away. (Joachim Hoelzgen)

The tent is still standing, but the storm gets under the edge of it and threatens to lift it off the ground. Friedl is crouched in the extreme corner, in an endeavour to hold it down. (Robert Schauer)

colours of the rising sun.
After initial difficulties, I now feel in fine form, ascend the snow slope to the right of the spur and finally climb onto a rib of rock. After every 50 metres of height, I have to put in a rest. I glance frequently at the altimeter.
In the rising wind one of the two tents at Camp I flutters violently. It tugs on its anchor like a hot air balloon. A gust of wind has plucked it from out of the ground, along with everything inside it. I must re-pitch it. Finally, at 11.30, one and a half hours after my arrival, I slump exhausted into the tent. Inside are the mats and radio apparatus.
Renato doesn't arrive for another two hours. The wind is still blowing and the tent fabric flaps. A snow flurry is blowing up. Renato is worried about the way he is acclimatising. He brings the subject into the conversation with increasing frequency.

29 June

Moments of Danger exercise the Mind

After a sleepless, stormy night in Camp II, Schauer and Mutschlechner retreat back down in continuing bad weather. Gogna and Casarotto remain in Camp I. (Joachim Hoelzgen)

The weather is bad. Renato and I wait it out. Robert and Friedl come down from Camp II during the snow squall. Friedl lends us his memo pad as he goes past. At 20.00 hours another storm sweeps in from the south. I sleep in my clothes. All night long we prop up the sides of the tent.
By morning, the wind has swung round, blowing predominantly from the north, from Sinkiang. It becomes increasingly fierce. We lie there apathetically, our heads against the tentpoles, dozing; we no longer care if the fabric rips or not. Renato writes in his notebook that he doesn't mind such moments of danger, for 'by experiencing them, the mind is exercised, it learns to work, discover and solve problems.' He sees fear as a kind of release-mechanism, 'enabling the body very quickly to develop the capability of saving itself.'
Up here at 6100 metres the wind sounds like the thunder of enormous avalanches, or the roar of a giant tidal wave; it is a very eerie situation. Cowering like a small child in a thunderstorm, I snuggle into my down sleeping bag.

30 June

Yet what can I say where no-one has my ears? (Friedrich Nietzsche)

At eight o'clock the weather conditions show clear signs of improvement. The wind is gradually easing. Hope returns of being able to continue climbing.
From rope to rope, we scramble upwards. We are carrying our personal equipment for a summit attempt, a big tent, the down sleeping bags, food for three days, stove and gas cartridges, radio, two first-aid tins. Too much! Renato is not up to the effort. I climb with him for a short while, then go on ahead.
I know that we can be seen by telescope from Base Camp as we emerge from the top of House's Chimney. Wearily I mount the last snow slope to the little Gore-tex tent. Once there, I lose no time in scooping out a place for a second tent. It will have the sheer drop on one side, ice and stones on the other.
Renato arrives at 17.00 hours. He has had to leave some of his load behind at 6300 metres. Now he is very tired. His toes are frozen and have lost all feeling. It is very alarming. Inside the tent it's not very comfortable. I have to lie with my head in the doorway as I need to be able to fetch in snow. The weight of my body presses against the side of the tent that juts

Gogna climbs alone to Camp II and Casarotto follows laboriously after. Gogna erects the two-man tent he has brought up with him. (Joachim Hoelzgen)

out into space. Between Renato and I there is hardly room for the stove. On top of all this I can only sleep if I reverse around and put my feet in the entrance shoving my sleeping mat closer to Renato. Inevitably I slide over onto the hollow side of the tent floor.

1 July

Nature cannot be commanded, she must be obeyed. (Francis Bacon)

By six o'clock I am already awake and busy preparing breakfast. Renato is reluctant to do anything. He says he will stay in camp and reorganise the tent. So I will go ahead and fix ropes on my own.
By the look of the banks of cloud to the west, I very much doubt if the weather will hold. At eight o'clock I radio my intentions to the others. Reinhold and Michl, who have just arrived in Camp I, listen in as well. I am glad that Reinhold commends my decision as a plucky one and hopes I will be able to do my best. I shoulder two coils of rope and start climbing. After the discovery of a metal ladder I find remains of ropes from the Japanese expedition. I have to be careful not to put too much weight on it; they're pretty rotten. I replace them with a section of my own rope, knotting the loose ends together. This way I make fairly rapid progress. At 6835 metres I leave one rope, pegs and karabiners behind.

In a biting wind, Gogna climbs 300 vertical metres up the iced rocks of the Black Pyramid. He replaces the defective Japanese fixed ropes with new rope and pegs. Casarotto stays behind in Camp II. Messner and Dacher move up from Base Camp to Camp I. (Joachim Hoelzgen)

Standing on an outcrop I can see Base Camp. The weather has definitely deteriorated. As I churn up snow with my feet, it is blown into my face by the wind. At 7000 metres I am left with no option but to retreat; it is already 12.15. I'll go a bit further tomorrow. Perhaps Renato will come with me.
Our radio link-up at 15.00 hours brings me congratulations – everyone says that I have completed an important task today. Glowing from their praise, I glance at Renato who is very discouraged, hardly eating and not drinking much either. Every success, it seems, is at the psychological cost of someone else!

2 July
No Dreams, no Signs

Gales and thick snowdrifts prohibit all upward progress. (Joachim Hoelzgen)

The next morning the sky is leaden. My élan of the previous day has evaporated. We decide between ourselves that after breakfast and the radio link-up, we will go down. We reach Camp I at 8.30 where Reinhold and Michl greet us with tea and crispbread spread with jam. They want to sit it out, but we continue on down and reach the glacier fairly tired, wearily working our way through the constantly changing pattern of seracs. We rope up.
With the strain of this, and the constant ever-present danger of falling into crevasses, the prospect of the summit is robbed of all interest. In the first place it will be much harder up there than here, and secondly, my only thought at the moment is to reach Base Camp and enjoy its comforts. Anyone who wants to climb K2 must be truly crazy! Step by step I trudge on; now that we are in sight of the people at Base Camp, I endeavour not to stumble too often.
In camp I conceal my pessimism. Only to Renato do I confide how very much I wish this expedition would come to an end. I sleep like a stone that night. For four days I have been in good health. Sadly, the same cannot be said for Renato. Robert, who has been in charge of our medical care since Ursula's departure, diagnoses that he has a mild attack of bronchitis. Coupled with diarrhoea, Renato's spirits are at absolute rock bottom. Yet notwithstanding, he cherishes greater hopes than I.

4 July

Glorious weather. Messner quickly scales the route prepared by Gogna on the Black Pyramid. Dacher follows him. They climb 400 metres above Gogna's high point, to reach 7300 m. Just before reaching the site for Camp III, they have to turn back because their rope has run out. Schauer and Mutschlechner go to Camp I. (Joachim Hoelzgen)

The extravagant praise for my solo climb surprises me. Reinhold congratulates me on my good work and courage. Certainly I'm very flattered to hear such an opinion, and perhaps I need it a bit. It's a pity that in my heart I don't feel so sure what the others really think about it. I no longer place my trust in myself, but in one who is greater than I. In him now rest all my hopes and beliefs. How can I expect him to let *me* climb to the summit of K2. How can I be sure that that's his plan for me? So far he has given me a free hand; maybe assisted me. But perhaps he has also put obstacles in my way. I see no signs, no omen; I feel only weariness after these energetic days. No dreams point the way. Perhaps the Other Side is tired of sending me messages I can't understand. Has it perhaps decided to give me up?
This dreadful waiting becomes purgatory for me. I don't place too much value on the praise of my comrades, although it flatters my pride. On the contrary, I would rather discover more about my true situation and take less notice of how the others see me.

5 July
Each his Possibility?

Messner and Dacher turn back to Base Camp. Schauer and Mutschlechner erect Camp II. Good weather with temperatures reaching fifteen degrees. (Joachim Hoelzgen)

Life in Base Camp is lazy. I don't emerge from my tent before 11 o'clock. It is no longer the perfect little homestead. The floor is all sloping because the glacier is grinding away underneath. It was no great problem as far as I was concerned, it didn't seem unendurable, but Renato asserted himself. Together with the porters he wants to put 'his house' in order.
So for a short time I have moved into Reinhold's tent; Reinhold with Michl has just climbed down from the Camp II area.
At midday yesterday they were within 50 metres of Camp II, when a slope at the end of the Black Pyramid halted progress. They had run out of rope. Erecting the camp, however, presents no other problem. Friedl and Robert, who have set off today, will do it.
Reinhold radiates confidence and infallibility. When shall I too be able to take pleasure in the climb, take pleasure in it being my turn to do the route-finding and press on ahead? Nor is Reinhold at all tired, seemingly. I let him tell me of his and Michl's climb, and how the last section, the Black Pyramid is difficult, steep and exposed. Reinhold is convinced, however, that Friedl and Robert will manage to establish the camp alright. That means that immediately afterwards we must think about a summit bid.
Discussion turns to the critical question: who will be the first? Strictly speaking, Renato and I are entitled to the next turn. But Renato is not yet recovered, nor am I ready. So it will have to be Reinhold and Michl who try it. The start is fixed for 8 July.

K2 is so terrible that it's as much a wonder today as it ever was if it's climbed at all. (Galen Rowell)

Then I bring up a tricky question with Reinhold; Renato listens:
'With no previous experience at 8000 metres, what can our rope do alone?'
Reinhold answers, 'It's not a question of 8000 metres. I am sure that any one of us not in a condition to reach the summit, will already have dropped out between 7000 and 7500 metres. I know that higher up the speed you climb will be reduced by half, but whoever can get up to the camp without being exhausted, is capable of going further. I'll give you a few tips if you want. Anyone who doesn't manage to get from Camp I to Camp II in four or five hours is out of the show; anyone who doesn't make it from Camp II to III

in six hours at most, would do better to turn back.'
Reinhold goes on: 'We shall leave everything behind in the bivouac at 8000 metres for whoever climbs up afterwards, that includes the down sleeping bags. Renato, if you don't want to make a start at eight o'clock, then set off as late as nine the day after us. Robert and Friedl, you go at ten. If anything should happen to one of us, the other can join up with the rope following.'
To me, too, this seems the best solution. This way everyone has his chance.

6 July

Schauer and Mutschlechner set up Camp III (7350 m) and return back to Camp II. (Joachim Hoelzgen)

K2 is not to be taken lightly. There is one essential difference between it and other mountains. On Mount Everest, for instance, the necessary equipment can be carried to 8500 metres. The Sherpas take care of all that. There is no outside help on K2 – not for us at least. This hasn't always applied. In 1939 Wiessner had Sherpas on his expedition; and the Italians who came here in 1954 had Hunza porters up to 8000 metres. So far as finding remnants of the Japanese fixed ropes goes, in 1954 the Italians must similarly have found some belonging to the Americans of 1953, and Wiessner probably found some from 1938. Well, alright, history repeats itself, although here it only concerns details that our predecessors would prefer forgotten.
Joachim, who has made notes of our discussions on climbing strategy, looks at the expedition postcard and, out of the blue, suddenly says; 'You know Sandro, really I prefer you with a beard.'
I replied that I had worn a beard for nine years, but for some reason had shaved it off briefly during the summer of 1977.
'Why?' Joachim wants to know.
'Because if I shaved, I would be forced to look at myself in the mirror each morning. Which is important.'
'Another Narcissus,' says Reinhold.
'Well OK, but what is narcissism? Tell me that,' I throw in.
'I only look in the mirror if I'm trimming my hair or my beard,' Terry remarks, 'I like to see if I'm cutting straight.'
'How often, for instance, do the Baltis pick up a mirror, I wonder, without having a special reason?'
'I think one looks in a mirror to see if one is always the same – and to see oneself from the outside,' Reinhold puts in. 'The more a person explores his inner self, the more he comes to see that he is made up of various people – men, and women too – and the more people he perceives within himself, the more anxious he becomes lest he will split apart, disappear entirely. So he has to reaffirm his oneness by regarding himself from the outside.'
Terry, meanwhile, has continued the discussion with Joachim. I only catch his last words, '. . . like Sandro, not religious.'
'Hey – what do you mean? I *am* religious,' I turn to them both.
'That's not the impression you give from what you say.'
'Well, I really am religious. I firmly believe in a God who has created the world, and is still creating, and who sometimes tells us something wrong, because he doesn't know exactly what he is doing,' I say.
'God is goodness and truth! Not anything else. He sees everything.'

Can *you* see through this tent?' asks Terry.
'No.'
'He can!'
'That's not the point! He can do everything – but that includes evil; he can't tell the difference. He is like a mother who gives birth to a child, but doesn't know what that child will grow into or what its destiny will be. It is the child's job to learn how and why he came into the world.'
'For a child to be born, you need a father too. How can you compare a mother with God?' Terry wants to know.
'God is at the same time father and mother, heaven and earth,' I answer.

8 July
Setting off from Camp

I was a warrior, but that is all over now; these are hard times for me. (Sitting Bull)

Ros Alí brings us tea at eight o'clock as usual. I am still sleepy. It's only after I've sipped some of the warm liquid that I say to Renato, 'You know, today is the eighth of July. It's exactly eleven years ago today that I soloed the Walker Spur.' Grinning, Renato stretches out his hand.
Reinhold and Michl have already left early this morning at five o'clock. Terry and Joachim were up to see them off. Tomorrow it will be the turn of Renato and I. I still don't feel that all the signs augur well for us: I'm well aware how far the summit still is, very far, and I would gladly stay down here in Base Camp.
Renato, too, doesn't appear to be in the best of form. Nonetheless we make all the necessary preparations. I adjust crampons, select what camera equipment I want to take, and pack a few medicines, including some weak sleeping pills. Everything is ready; the only thing lacking now is the eagerness to be off.
The weather is splendid, it looks as if it will stay that way.

9 July
The North Wind

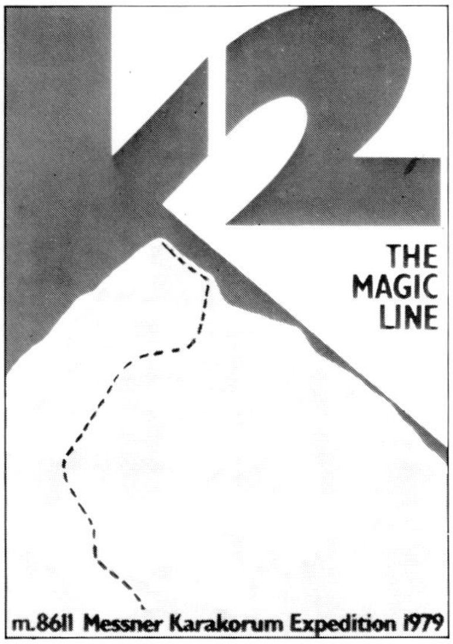

K2 Poster with the route that was originally intended.

As we are going up the glacier, Gulam Mahdi, who is to accompany Renato and I to Camp I, doesn't feel well. He has to keep disappearing behind boulders of ice.
During one of these stops, Ros Alí wanders off, climbs a rock, and comes back with a flower for me. I stick it in my hat. These little flowers grow at a height of 5300 metres, they are violet in colour with a light fragrance. A pure delight.
When we reach 5400 metres, Gulam finally collapses altogether. We wrap him up well. Ros Alí will take him back to Base Camp. Then Renato says he doesn't want to come any further either, he'll go down as well.
'Why?' I ask him.
'I seem to be all uncoordinated, not moving properly,' he answers.
It is his decision. So that's it. I'll go on alone and wait for Robert and Friedl in Camp I. I reach the camp at 8.30.
Reinhold and Michl have meanwhile left Camp II. Disturbing news comes up from Base Camp. The first contingent of the French expedition has arrived, ready to attempt our original objective, the 'Magic Line'. All very capable mountaineers, from the leader, Bernard Mellet, his deputy, Yannick Seigneur, down to Ivan Ghirardini, Patrick Cordier, Jean-Marc Boivin. . . .
Robert's wife, Kathi, has also arrived with the Frenchmen. She came up the Baltoro Glacier with an Austrian expedition and then joined the French group.

During the night a strong north wind gets up on the Abruzzi Rib. However, I am no longer frightened that the tent will take off, although I do keep waking up because everything round me is jumping about. I am suddenly impatient to get going on the real adventure. Perhaps my new-found confidence comes from the north wind, whispering to me to put my best foot forward. I think of the French expedition, the way Terry announced their arrival: 'It's like an earthquake: they are shaking the whole moraine.'

10 July
Do I really want it?

At 7.25 I hear wheezing outside the tent. Someone has arrived: it is Friedl. Half an hour later Robert is here as well. We all have breakfast together. I'm very fed up that the pair of them didn't think to bring my mail with them, which Kathi had brought in from Rawalpindi. But I make excuses for them and stifle what it would be better perhaps to say. I don't really believe in mere forgetfulness, and I keep racking my brains for reasons why Robert and Friedl should want to injure me in this way. And in so doing, I lose contact with reality and with both of them. If it goes on like this, I'll be my own worst enemy.

Upon the mountain of my fear I climb. (Wystan H. Auden)

In the expectation of worse days and nights ahead, I take pains to enjoy my stay in this camp. The prospect of the adventure ahead excites me. And Robert and Friedl even more so, they are more impatient than I. I try my hardest not to think too much about the next day, but I don't succeed. I would have liked to blame fate for the fear I feel, but really I am afraid of showing weakness. For me this world of huge mountains is like a town full of blind alleyways. Everything is poised to destroy my frail existence. Did I really believe in the beauty, the nobility, the adventure? Or is this climb not rather a nightmare, a witches' sabbath, an inferno, a vision of hell. Do I really want to get to the top of K2? Once up there, would I have sufficient energy left to develop positive pictures from the negative images of the world at my feet? Do I really like my companions? Am I the only one who frequently imagines the others perishing dramatically, tragically, whilst I return famous? Am I perhaps mad? Who are these bodies I can hear breathing heavily beside me, and taking up so much room in the tent?

11 July

I can admit to you that I fear death. Not what we imagine about death, for such fear is itself imaginary . . . But that death I suffer every moment, the death of that voice which, out of the depths of my childhood, keeps questioning me as it does you. 'Who am I?' Everything in and around us seems to conspire to strangle it once and for all. Whenever that voice is silent – and it doesn't speak often – I'm an empty body, a perambulating carcass. I'm afraid that one day it will fall silent forever, or that it will speak too late . . .
(René Daumal, *Mount Analogue*)

This is a decisive day for our expedition. Reinhold and Michl set off for Camp III. They take only one little tent, two down sleeping bags, a cooker and a few provisions. At 12 o'clock they are at 7800 metres, at 13.00 they have reached 7900 metres. They stop and set up their bivouac on much the same spot where in 1954 Walter Bonatti and the porter Mahdi had to spend the night out without a tent, some 80 metres below where Compagnoni and Lacedelli were camping. We follow on up to Camp II. It's all familiar ground. We climb without undue exertion. I am feeling fine and the afternoon slips by happily in the tent with me inventing ever more exotic fish soups.
Perhaps things don't go so well for Reinhold and Michl in their assault tent, but I don't want to think about that. And if for a moment, I get a flash of their situation, like some imaginary photograph, I don't suffer any disquiet on their behalf. The image slowly fades without leaving behind any agonising questions like, 'What if it were me?'

Going outside in the last glow of day, I am treated to a spectacular sunset: the sombre rock hulk of Masherbrum stands out clearly against the red flush on the horizon; the fiery red above the roof top of Chogolisa ebbs away like ink on blotting paper. I lose myself in the chilly embrance of this living, lambent, benign vastness, where everything is already written.

12 July
The Disappointed and the Debarred

Friedl, Robert and I get started at 7.15 on the section where the first fixed rope is. At nine we pass my previous highest point, the 7000 metres I reached a few days ago.
In several places the rope is a bit dangerous. At 11.15 I clamber up a last steep ice wall and stop in the hope of seeing over the top a view other than the wildly rugged panorama we have grown used to, a panorama into which within the last hour the distant but imposing figure of Nanga Parbat has appeared. Skiang Kangri and wide stretches of Tibet lie to the north and south below us. Also, I can see the tent which is our Camp III. At 15.00 hours we call up Base Camp on the radio to see how high Reinhold and Michl have got. No news yet.
Then at 17.10 we hear Michl over the radio ordering flowers for his wife from the summit! There follows an excited conversation with Base Camp, but I can only pick up a lot of crackling and cannot understand it at all. My sole thoughts now are for their descent and I pray it goes well. I suddenly imagine them falling and being killed and shudder violently. Anxiously I look at the long strip of cloud which marks the horizon to the south. Robert does nothing to allay my fears by saying it is only the monsoon over Rawalpindi.
I lie awake while my two companions snore. The night is very quiet, too quiet for my liking. None of the eagerly-awaited dreams, no portents. Perhaps my time has not come yet? Perhaps I still have some growing to do before I am ready?

Man is born with labour
And birth is but a hazard cast with death.
Even from his earliest breath
He suffers pain; mother and father both
Are from the first intent
To comfort him that he was ever born.
(Giacomo Leopardi, *Night Song*)

13 July
Strange Encounter

Friday the thirteenth. There is a 'smell' of bad weather in the air as we rise. The altimeter reads 60 metres more than yesterday, and there is a sneaky feeling of uncertainty hanging heavily over everything. Despite this we set about our preparations. The usual ceremonial. At seven o'clock we start climbing a seemingly endless snow slope. The ground is uneven and we never know from one moment to the next whether it will hold or suddenly cave in. Every time we do break through the surface, we stumble and it costs energy. We take it in turns to go out in front. The weather continues to worsen. It is hard to make out the shape of the others, even at five metres.
At nine o'clock we hear a shout above us. Reinhold and Michl! We call back excitedly.
'Where are you?'
'Here – coming straight down above you.'
And their position is confirmed as little pellets of snow roll down onto us. Shortly afterwards two figures lurch towards us through the murk, their beards stiff with ice. We hug them. I am so overcome I find myself weeping. Whether it's from joy at seeing them again, alive and victorious, or because I already know in my own mind that we will have to turn back, I don't know. We exchange very few words, yet this encounter at 7600 metres

No-one was to be a beast of burden for the others; all three ropes were to follow each other to the summit. When, as it proved, only one was successful – Dacher and Messner – this, nevertheless, represented a new high-point in the history of K2. For the first time a small expedition reached the summit, climbing in alpine style and completely without oxygen apparatus. (Wilhelm Bittorf)

makes a lasting impression.
Back in Camp III I quickly prepare a soup in the general chaos. Then we hurtle out into the storm, headfirst, leaving our gear behind, in an effort to get lower down the mountain. Reinhold and Michl are in astonishing form. They certainly don't show any signs of having just climbed the second highest mountain in the world.
We reach Camp II, where, meanwhile, Renato has arrived. He has tea ready and after a rest, we continue going down.

14 July

The champion of peace is debarred from inventing a sort of dummy figure of evil for the purpose of arousing the militant enthusiasm or strengthening the bond between the fighters for a good cause. To attack just 'evil' is a questionable procedure, even with intelligent people.
(Konrad Lorenz – *On Agression*)

Gulam Mahdi is to take our mail to Skardu. It includes a letter from Reinhold to Mr Aswan asking for permission to attempt Broad Peak. What incredible shape these two are in, Reinhold and Michl. Hardly back from the summit of K2 than already thinking about their next eight-thousander. Renato, Friedl, Robert and I take a dim view of, what we consider, this unjustifiable request. We hope Mr Aswan won't grant it.
I haven't had time to collect my thoughts yet and chew over these latest happenings. Since yesterday I have wanted to be content with the others' success. But I still have the feeling things are not finished yet. The weather is fine. Stars twinkle outside. The Milky Way glows. Reinhold says point-blank that as four, we stand less chance of making it than three – meaning without Renato. He waits for Renato to withdraw as he says that not everyone is equally strong at altitude, and it's no tragedy if someone doesn't make it. I have the impression that no-one else realises what Reinhold is getting at. But it's superfluous anyway. Renato has already given up.
At 23.00 Renato and I are in our tent. My rucksack is still unpacked. After a short silence Renato speaks. It's a sour business. I admire Renato's inner strength; he convinces himself that there will be other chances to make up for things in the future. He says, as if he meant it, that all things considered, this expedition has been a useful experience, opening his eyes to new perspectives and he has begun to learn how to relate to other people. All the same he hadn't expected the price to be so high. Secretly he had seen himself as a second Reinhold – that was all over now.

More even than the success of Messner and Dacher, the failure of the other three demonstrates how much luck, but also how much instinct and inner capacity for speed, are all part of the process of 'bagging' the monster, K2. (Wilhelm Bittorf)

15 and 16 July
Old, Familiar Fear

Messner waits until all the other members of the expedition have also made their bid for the summit.
(Joachim Hoelzgen)

I feel light and supple, my pace is even. Friedl and Robert leave me behind at the first fixed rope, but I don't care. It's a beautiful morning and the rocks are dry. I can almost always manage to place my foot where there is no snow lying.
In Camp I everything is still alright. Robert has the stove going by the time I arrive, Friedl is busying himself with his 'housework' in the little Gore-tex tent. It's only eight o'clock. The day's not over for us yet. After a good brew, we want to climb on up to Camp II. That way we can save a day, but it will mean 1800 metres of altitude in a single go – can we manage it?
I arrive at Camp II at 12.30, not quite as exhausted as I had feared. Here, too, the tents are alright. I remember that somewhere here Renato has dumped some provisions. Over the radio I ask him where he put them. We dine excellently.
The next day after three and a half hours we reach Camp III only to find

that the wind has ripped the flysheet and the titanium tent pole has snapped. Once repaired, it seems to us that the tent is better than before, if rather less stable without its fly. The band of mist on the horizon and the mass of cloud over Sinkiang as the sun goes down, doesn't presage well. All the old familiar fears start up again. I am tormented by a longing for security. That is the real reason why the night before a big climb, I am always so miserable.

17 and 18 July
Fate and Freedom

All your seasick sailors, they are rowing home.
All your reindeer armies, are all going home.
The lover who just walked out your door
Has taken all his blankets from the floor.
The carpet, too, is moving under you
And it's all over now, Baby Blue.
(Bob Dylan)

The weather is unsettled. Insidious banners of cloud mask the summits of Broad Peak and Chogolisa; K2 seems to be stifled in mist. Nevertheless, we set off, firmly resolved to reach the bivouac under the summit. Once above the Shoulder, the cloud is so thick that we cannot make out the little tent at the celebrated Bonatti Bivouac. With the aid of altimeters and instinct we finally reach the wretched tent in a strong wind.
Everything is iced up, snow forces its way in everywhere. It is a work of art, fitting three of us into the one tent, and still finding room to cook. Sleeping will be even worse.
The wind, blowing in from the south, lashes the tent all night. Friedl's feet, wrapped in his down sleeping bag, rest on my shoulders, and my feet on his. We are forced to spend many hours in the same position without moving. Every inch of our bodies ache.
At 6.30 I step outside the tent. Devilish cold! I am greeted by relentless gusts of wind. Visibility is bad. All the elements seem to have been set loose. I wonder if we will be able to get down in time? Inside the tent Robert and Friedl are tying themselves into knots putting on their gaiters and stormproof clothing. I keep hoping the conditions will improve. My fingers freeze to my crampons; beard and eyelashes are caked with ice.
Descent is inevitable, and we must move fast. Step by step we struggle down through the brittle, crusty, snow, pelted by icy showers of hail.
Reinhold has managed to extend the period of the expedition. We ought still to have a chance, he tells us over the radio. The porters have been ordered for 29 July, so we can make a summit attempt up until 24 July.
It is already dark when we arrive back in base. In my heart I already know this is the end, but I don't want to believe it yet.

19 and 20 July
Michl shakes his Head

The unconquerable Odysseus looked down on them with a scowl. 'You curs!' he cried, 'You never thought to see me back from Troy!'
(Odyssey XXII)

Very few incidents mark these two recuperative days. But all the time the cancer of doubt gnaws away in secret. And the bad weather gets me down.
In the afternoon of the nineteenth I have a long chat with Reinhold. We discuss the various ways of looking at life and exercising control over it. I am glad to find that we can continue to share common aims in the future. What I admire about Reinhold is his natural flair for living intuitively and adventurously, his freedom of choice. This is my way, too, although perhaps I approach it from a more intellectual viewpoint.
I sleep almost without interruption. Reinhold lies in the sun. Michl shakes his head at me, from which I am given to understand that he thinks I have changed, and not for the better. I am not offended. He has his reasons. Besides I can sense just how much altruistic affection leads him to express this.
Reinhold is unsure how much he ought to say about the current position. The fact that we three are not at all convinced that we are capable of

getting to the top, is not his problem. During the evening we decide to set off at three the next day.
When it comes to climbing a mountain like K2, there is no room for bluff or lies. It takes every bit of my experience as an alpinist as well as all my physical strength to solve the difficulties of the route.

21 July
Freedom of Choice?

Ros Alí comes to call me at three in the morning.
'Sandro Sahib, tea making? Today going?' he asks in his fractured English.
I look up at the sky, where already half the stars have disappeared, and swear under my breath. Why does Ros Alí bring this question to me, and not Robert? In the weak half-light I step outside and stagger stiff-legged over the stones. First impressions confirm that this, the first day under Leo (my star sign), is pretty much as expected. At breakfast, morosely chewing on a French toast, Robert admits he feels awful, and Friedl, although with his blue eyes and thick blond beard shining in the candlelight might look very Viking-like, he shows nothing of the Viking spirit today. The summit is not visible. Clouds enwrap the flanks of the mountain. It is warm, but even so all the glacier rubble is coated over with a smooth layer of ice.
As we leave, I turn round and see Michl with his head sticking out of his tentflap. He doesn't shout any greeting, but we nod at each other. Just past the French Camp stomach cramps force me to stop. I ask Robert for a tablet, then keep going only with great effort. It is as if some giant hand were pressing me into the ground and not allowing me to breathe. Everything in me screams to turn back. I grit my teeth and ask myself quite seriously what it is that drives me on.
The weather is dreadful. I have lost any inclination to go on – the expedition has been successful after all. But my pride-cloaked ego relentlessly urges me to keep climbing; and fear, too, adds its voice, telling me it would be cowardice to stop now. Two figures keep going ahead of me. I hope that one of them will change his mind; though I doubt if I could accept this assistance in coming to my own decision. It seems I'm not able to turn back in the wake of someone else.
With a dull droning, an avalanche comes down our route. Had we set off half an hour earlier, we should have come to grief in its air-blast. Yet another of those portentious signs! My left foot breaks through the crust of snow and splashes in water underneath. To be able to relinquish all hopes of success – vain and fantastic as any such hope is – I have to turn back of my own volition. Only by retreating along my own footsteps can I win my inward struggle. And the price is that in future I must not attach real importance to things, but be satisfied with what fate deals. I still cling to the illusion that the weather is going to improve, that the hours in the high camps will somehow fly away, that the tiredness I feel doesn't exist.
Now my right foot, too, plunges into a waterhole. I let out a yell. The other two stop. Ros Alí, grasping the situation immediately, hands me the pair of spare boots he is carrying for me. Is that all there is to it? Is release so easy? How weightless my steps are going back! How bright the monsoon sun, which for a moment lightens my lonely way back into Base Camp.

Everything all around is deathlike, and so bleak that one might really prefer to fall into a glacier crevasse. Scarcely any wind, no clouds. In the grey of the mist, not a human soul anywhere. A real Hell, for a living being. Each of us lies alone in his tent, reading, writing. Out of sheer boredom we concoct fancy things to eat. Twice a day we crawl outside our tiny homesteads. (Reinhold Messner)

27 July

The Justice of K2

There is no peace, in the sense in which you mean it. No doubt there is a peace, but not that peace which abides, and never forsakes us. On earth there is only that peace which we must conquer over and over again, from day to day, in ever fresh assaults and victories.
(Herman Hesse, *Narziss and Goldmund*)

Reinhold lies in the sun. Michl pours me some tea. These two very different personalities have been to the summit of K2, and from there spoken to the world.

I am sure that the experience hasn't altered them, nor will it. For a reason I haven't yet fathomed, the summit, for them is not important, and still less are all the honours. They, who dispense tea like oriental priests and doze in the sun after the great adventure, are possessed of an inner strength that keeps them pure. I can't divine exactly what goes on inside them, but the loose pieces inside me have dovetailed together. The exertion, the cold, the thin air were silent witnesses to this process.

K2 is the only theatre in the world where the play *Justice* is enacted. In that airy courtroom, there are no statute books, lawyers, or advocates; there is only fire, earth, air, water, gold-coloured insects, fearful monsters, flowers with eight petals, saints, murderers, powerful mandala, God and the Devil. And all these elements have one single energy. It flows into the strings which hold the two puppets on the stage. The sum of all the energy operates the strings into movement, into a climb which seems destined never to end. The art of the marionettes is to submit to this energy. The discovery is shattering. We are the marionettes, and as spectators we follow the film in which we are the performers. Edgar Allan Poe said that everything we see or seem, is nothing more than a dream within a dream.

Reinhold and I stand gazing up at this mighty mountain. From here, it looks easier and less steep than it did. I say it's probably because of some curvature of space which we can't explain.

Turning to go into the tent, I feel propelled by an undeniable yet agreeable force – as in a storm, I am flung into the heart of the mountain. And here the vision of another world is revealed to me: Everything is changed, everything pleasantly distorted; it is the veils that are missing.

'That is Reality,' I say, but the vision in the heart of the magic mountain has gone . . . Did I dream it?

Leave your stepping stones behind, something calls for you,
Forget the dead you've left, they will not follow you.
The vagabond who's rapping at your door
Is standing in the clothes that you once wore.
Strike another match, go start anew
And it's all over now, Baby Blue.
(Bob Dylan)

March to Base Camp

The famous monsoon – the warm, moist south-west wind which brings the great rains to India – reaches the Karakorum in a greatly attenuated form. It discharges much of its moisture on to the smaller chains and on to the plateaux which constitute the outposts of the Karakorum and which, at least in part, represent the true western continuation of the Himalaya. The Karakorum has less rain than the rest of the Himalaya and consequently, even below the climatic limit of the permanent snows, is very bare and in many places little more than a desert. This is more markedly the case on the northern than on the southern side. (Ardito Desio)

But the climatic differences between the Everest group and the Karakorum are also due in part to the fact that the two groups are situated at different distances from the sea. The highest peak of the Karakorum, K2, is more than 900 miles inland. Everest, on the other hand, is only 400 miles from the coast. That is why the great forests which clothe the southern slopes of the Nepalese Himalaya up to a considerable altitude are not duplicated on the southern slopes of the Karakorum. We have to travel much farther south to find their counterpart – to the southernmost tip, in fact, of that magnificent mountain region which bears the name of Kashmir. (Ardito Desio)

In the Karakorum vegetation is found at far higher altitudes than in the Alps. Moss and lichen flourish at more than 6500 m, and even occasional tufts of grass are to be seen at altitudes exceeding 5500 m. Where there is grass there are always a few small brightly-coloured flowers which in summer peep from the midst of heaps of stones or from crevices in the rocks – among them saxifrage, primulas, gentian, campanulas and even edelweiss, identical in appearance with those found in the Alps. These flowers sometimes form carpets of many colours at the edge of patches of grass. (Ardito Desio)

I often feel here, as if we were living between worlds, between times. As if the old times were past and the new not yet dawned. (Reinhold Messner)

Right: The march in to Base Camp usually takes two to three weeks. The porters have to be cared for medically, partly equipped and completely fed. To keep them moving all day and then at night to keep control of the loads, is a job calling for skill, a lot of patience, and a sympathetic understanding of their way of life.

Below: The route from Skardu to Base Camp is not just arduous, involving as it does the dangerous passage through the Braldo Gorge and climbing forty-four miles over the rubble and ice of the Baltoro and Godwin-Austen Glaciers. In the higher regions it is impossible to obtain any firewood; and in spring the whole route is frequently under deep snow.

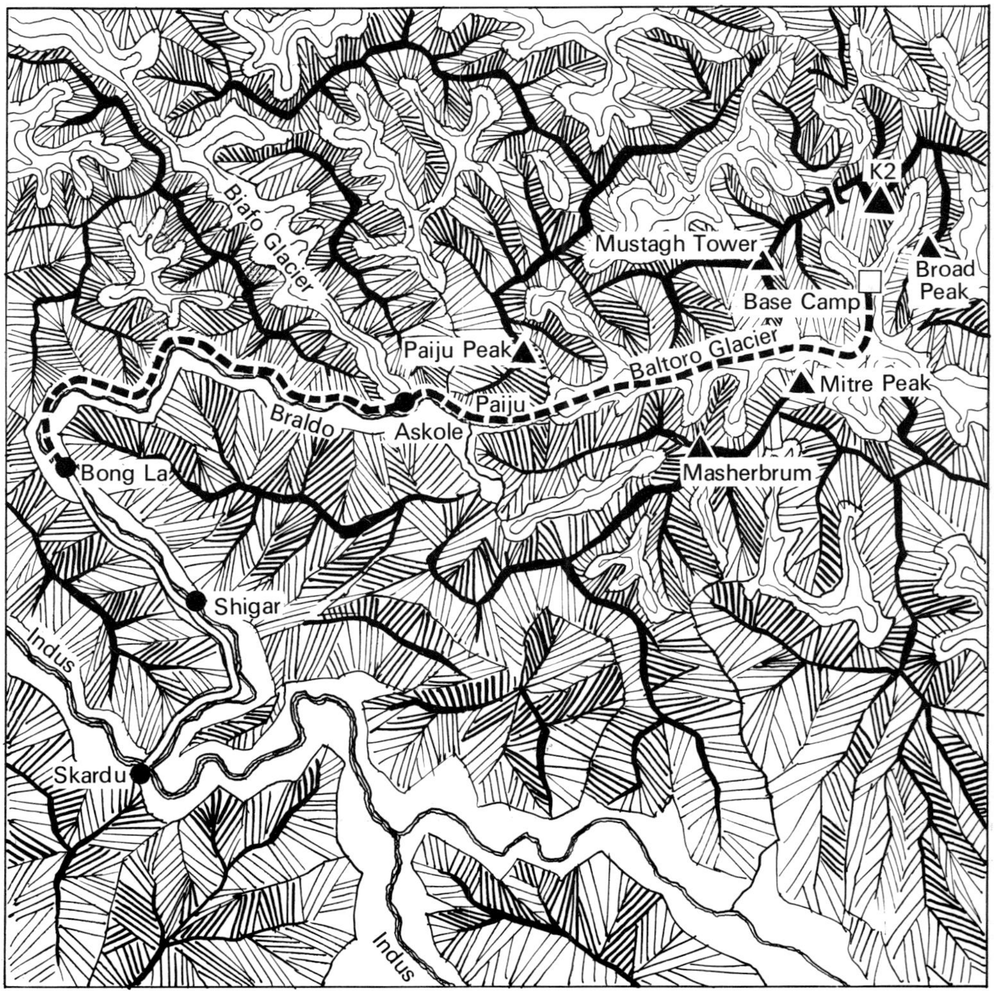

I feel a deep, unshakable affection towards the porters. Even travelling these valleys alone, I never feel lonely.
(Reinhold Messner)

In the Karakorum a porter will carry an average load of 25 kilograms. On top of that he will have his own personal belongings: a blanket, a cooking pot, spices – and hashish. In Skardu the expedition selects 136 men from the 500 who offer themselves as porters,

I go up there to learn, to talk with the people about the winds and the mountains and distances. And what I know, I know from them. (Reinhold Messner)

The stretch between Skardu and Bong La is covered by tractors and jeeps; the long convoy transports the three tons of expedition equipment as well as the porters. Once in Bong La the loads are divided amongst the porters. One has to carry the great swaying bundle of foam rubber mats which gives him a lot of trouble on the difficult rock passages.

To find adventure on a tame planet, the children of comfort plunge themselves into ever more bizarre escapades.
(Wilhelm Bittorf)

I cannot submit myself to anyone's authority, nor do I want people to be subjected to my authority. So I find it very difficult to be expedition leader.
(Reinhold Messner)

Perhaps this dread of transience explains our greed for the few gobbets of raw experience in modern life.
(Peter Matthiessen)

The Braldo Gorge is the most dangerous section of the approach march to K2. The porters are under constant threat from stonefalls, and the path is so steep and loose that in places they have to scramble on all fours.

The craving for adventure atrophies, not simply because it is like some organ which no longer serves any purpose, but because there are no unexplored continents left and no more conquests to make.
(Wilhelm Bittorf)

Striding along, my body becomes so highly-charged it would be quite impossible for me to stop. It feels as if something wants to break free, to burst from my breast. It is a surge of longing that carries me forward as if I were possessed. (Reinhold Messner)

K2
K2

In Chongo and Chakpo the expedition camps lie on the outskirts of the village. The local farmers sell us eggs and sour milk (lassi). The women usually keep out of sight except for little girls who venture up and down to the camp.

Any sense of awkwardness between me and the people around me vanishes as I become absorbed into this region. As if I were in meditation, I grow into this world, and, in peace, see it more clearly.
(Reinhold Messner)

A good hour's march beyond Askole at the foot of the Mango Gusar, Ursula Grether, the expedition doctor, slips and falls. She damages her ankle so badly that it is impossible for her to carry on. In desperation the team try to make radio contact with the outside world while the porters look on disinterestedly. Finally, Reinhold Messner and Friedl Mutschlechner carry Ursula back to Askole.

We have no option but to continue without a doctor. I accept the challenge and think no more about it. (Reinhold Messner)

A mania for safety tends to cripple the spirit. For that reason we become fascinated with adventure, as a prisoner is with freedom.
(Reinhold Messner)

The expedition progresses through icily cold Karakorum rivers, across the boulder fields of the Braldo, whose water level, now in springtime, is still low.

A sense of space emerges from the jumble of simultaneous and contradictory thoughts in my head. I feel things are getting clearer. Time no longer exists.
(Reinhold Messner)

Next double page: The column of porters toils endlessly up and down the churned-up, rubble-strewn Baltoro Glacier. It is four day's march to Concordia, the last campsite before Base Camp.

During the day the heat on the boulder wastes is unbearable; the temperature rises to 50°C and more. The men thirstily gulp from little glacier lakes. In Paiju the porters take on extra loads of wood so that they can cook chapatis and brew tea on the hostile Baltoro Glacier.

I journey onwards at peace with myself and full of enthusiasm for this landscape. I love this trampled, boulder-strewn river of ice and am glad to be here. I imagine myself dead, and flowing down the valley entombed in this ice, and the prospect makes me content with life, and with death.
(Reinhold Messner)

Above Urdukas the expedition enters the realms of snow. At first just the debris of dead glaciers, but higher up the mantle is continuous. When the sun softens it, climbers and porters find themselves wading waist-deep in the snow. The caravan frequently pauses to rest.

As in a dream torn from the march, I turn my thoughts towards civilisation. And I see myself beset by an emptiness, which fills everything around me to as far as I can see. (Reinhold Messner)

K2

The Balti porters spend the night wrapped up in their woollen blankets lying under a tarpaulin. Going to bed means a lot of hard work for them, digging stones out of the ice to make a level platform. Barefoot, as laid down in the Koran, they pray to Allah at sunrise and sunset, but thinking all the time of the wages they will receive once in Base Camp. It will amount to over 1000 rupees per man – equivalent to a whole year's income in this mountain area, earned in just three weeks of heavy load-carrying.

What is climbing? Curiosity, doubts, privation, enthusiasm – and faith.
(Pete Schoening)

Each evening a chorus of chanting can be heard echoing around the Godwin-Austen Glacier. It is the Balti porters at prayer. Their voices fade gradually into the distance till they are nothing more than a muffled lament. (Renato Casarotto)

From the campsite at Concordia the route follows the Godwin-Austen Glacier to the foot of K2, crossing little rivulets which have eaten their way through the ice, and over endless fields of granular snow. Even at this distance K2 dominates the whole region like some mystical pyramid.

The feeling sometimes comes to me that I have already died and therefore have nothing left to lose. It washes over me in the early mornings when I awake from a restless, dreamless sleep. I busy myself and feel inwardly calm and content. Nothing worse can happen to me. (Reinhold Messner)

From the place where earlier K2 attempts had their base, the Messner expedition plans by passing between the Savoia Glacier and the southern slopes of the Angelus to gain the bottom of the West Flank (right). This plan has to be changed when a porter is killed falling into a crevasse. They turn back to the Base Camp on the Godwin-Austen Glacier, where 25 years ago the first climbers to scale K2 set up their tents.

Climbing for me is like practising a religion: it helps me to a new relationship with the world, to an understanding of that world and of myself and the way I fit into it.
(Reinhold Messner)

The memorial cairn on K2, built for Art Gilkey in 1953. It also bears the names of those lost in 1939 as well as Mario Puchoz, all inscribed on aluminium plaques.

The dramatic history of K2 reads like a saga: in 1939 four men were lost, in 1953 almost the whole team fell from just under the Shoulder (large picture); Mario Puchoz died in 1954 on the Abruzzi Rib; Nick Estcourt in 1978 under an avalanche; and in 1979 a porter on the South Ridge. Knowing in advance of the storms which beset this exposed peak, along with the fact that above the Shoulder any hope of rescue for a small team in the event of an emergency is practically out of the question, in moments of semi-consciousness can build up to disquiet, indeed even to fear. (Reinhold Messner)

Once in Base Camp, many of the rigours, dangers and worries lay behind us. Ahead is the climb up to the notorious Death Zone, and the daily struggle with one's own doubts and lethargy.
(Reinhold Messner)

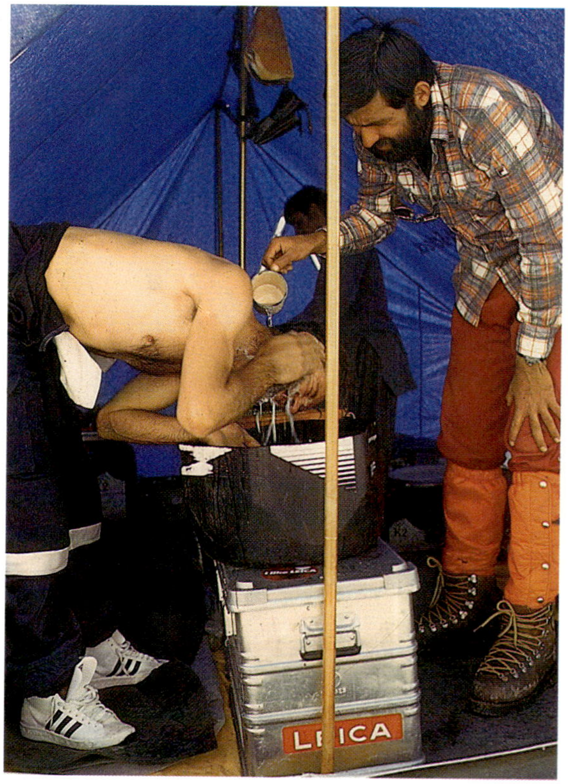

Base Camp is situated on the bend of the Godwin-Austen Glacier, where coming down from the direction of Windy Gap it curves south towards Concordia. Six sleeping tents and a cook tent are established. The cook tent doubles as a living and wash-room.

The Pakistani Liaison Officer Mohammed Tahir, known as Terry (above right) is a fully-integrated member of the expedition. Always ready with help and sympathy, he proves himself also to be an excellent cook.

Now that I live mostly alone, my self-assurance and the knowledge of who I am, hinges upon my day-to-day environment: the heaviness of the air, the atmosphere with my friends, the terrain on which I pitch my tent, the height of the mountains around me.
(Reinhold Messner)

Left: In a matter of weeks, the snow which at the start covered Base Camp, melts away. Soon the tents are standing on heaps of stones, a metre or so high. The ice creaks and moans, and since the time a crevasse with water in the bottom, opened up under Reinhold Messner's tent, his dreams frequently involve falling into crevasses.

The present-day configuration of the Karakorum is the result of a complex series of transformations to which the region was subjected after its final emergence from the sea. Under the impulse of powerful orogenic thrusts the strata which make up this narrow strip of the earth's crust were first bent and broken, then compressed and heaped one upon the other, and finally raised to an enormous height. Meanwhile, this vast area of super-elevation was attacked by atmospheric agencies which were responsible for the appearance of the first valleys. (Ardito Desio)

During this expedition my self-confidence centres around the fact that I know with certainty that we are coming here because we must. (Reinhold Messner)

Through the months of travel and experience, including deeply personal experience, this wilderness soothes me. Despite all its visible and destructive energy, I feel safe. (Reinhold Messner)

I grow more at peace in a direct ratio to the noise the wind makes outside the tent and amongst the stones. (Reinhold Messner)

At the beginning my constantly-recurring dream is of being hustled around continuously: going up and down in lifts, shuttled from place to place. In my loneliness and solitude I continually look for escape routes. (Reinhold Messner)

The view of the Baltoro is breathtaking and fascinating in the extreme. From such a vantage point the glacier appears as a colossal, I would almost say monstrous, river of ice that fills the valley as the sea fills a fiord. It is the image of what our great alpine valleys must have looked like during the Ice Age. In the background rises the enormous pyramid of K2, while at the sides can be seen those other colossi of the Karakorum, Broad Peak and the four Gasherbrums with their satellites. (Ardito Desio)

Below: Base Camp, situated between Broad Peak and K2 on the dead strips of glacier which have embedded themselves like a motorway between both of the main ice flows of the Godwin–Austen Glacier.

———	Approach route
– – – –	Dacher/Schauer reconnaissance
. . . .	Messner/Mutschlechner reconnaissance
— — —	Abruzzi Ridge route

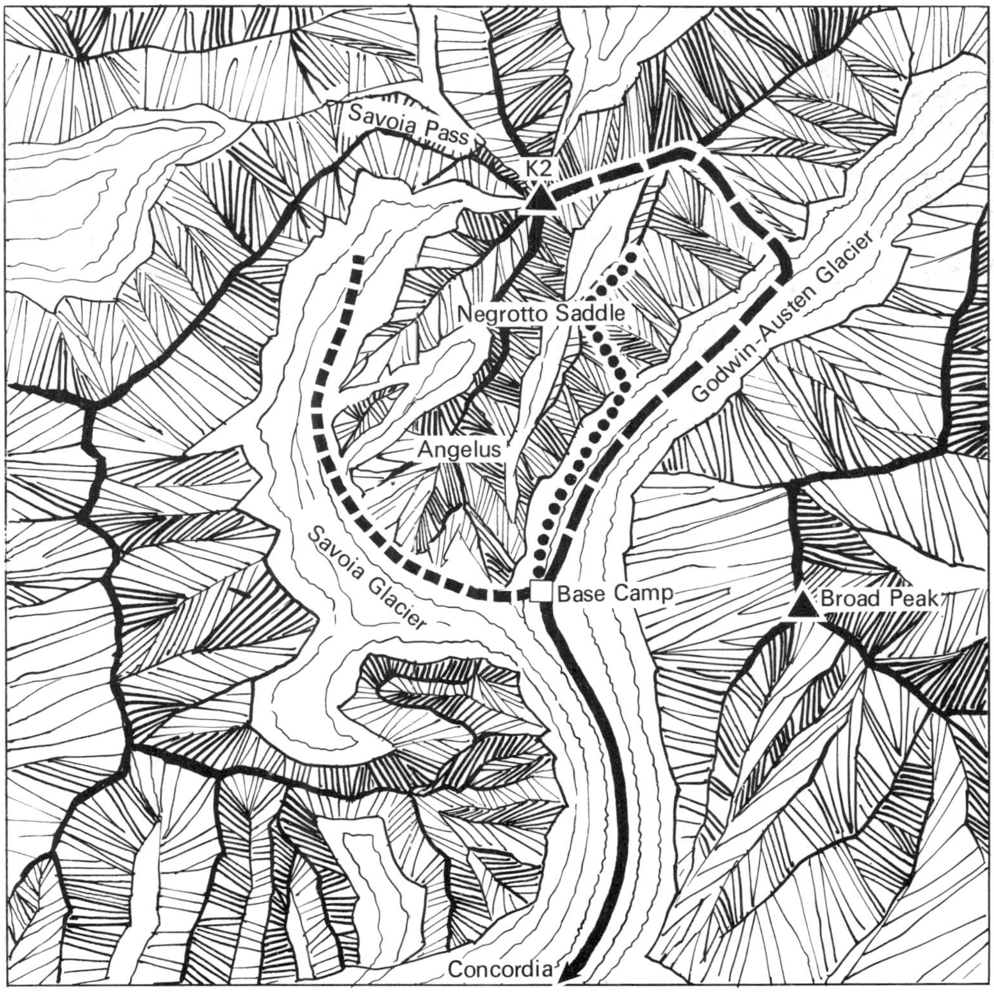

The Shadow of K2

It is afternoon, still pleasantly warm, when I shake out my rucksack in front of the tent. A few of the ravens which lurk around Base Camp like highway robbers, take a few hops nearer. I squat inside the tent. All the items of equipment I need for a summit bid are lying in an ordered jumble on my sleeping mattress. I am the only one who could see any logic in this chaos of clothes, boots and laces. Item by item, I arrange them carefully in the blue sack, test the weight, pack some more.

7 July

Looking at the summit from Base Camp, in its dizzy remoteness, not infrequently triggers within me that feeling, at the same time both uplifting and disturbing of being far, far away. (Reinhold Messner)

As I squirm into the fresh air again, the great black birds fly back with hoarse croaks. A gust of wind catches the group and scatters them. They soar off in different directions. One goes so high that for a moment he is poised in a direct line with the summit of K2. I think, don't go higher than the summit; and as I look up, he flaps back down. He's like me, that raven, pushing himself beyond his own horizon.

I open the rucksack once more to make sure I haven't forgotten anything. This is our first attempt on the summit. Holding the items in my hand, constantly-changing images flash before me, fading from one to the next, like a kind of lantern show. Picking up the crampons, I have a vision of blank blue-green ice; the gloves conjour up night cold; the little assault-tent, the frosty air of the death zone.

Sitting back inside the tent, I hear a sound like someone grumbling, and then a clatter of stones. Michl peers in and asks if by chance I have a second pair of gloves he can have. As I hand them over, I can see he's very pleased, but he just nods and goes back to his own tent and his rucksack. I can hear him busying himself with it. For all his air of calm and dependability, Michl is ambitious and keen to make the attempt. The majority of the route has already been prepared and we two have learned the measure of each other. Even during the weeks of preparation, we found ourselves in accord and it was tacitly agreed between us that we would attempt the summit together. We work well together, but we are not sworn partners.

Half an hour later my rucksack is packed and I stand it outside the tent, twice more lifting it up to test its weight. 'So,' I say to myself – just that 'So', as if it had some meaning.

During the course of the day, the dull haze which has hung heavy in the air since dawn, gradually evaporates, and the layer of mist moves away eastwards. Windows of blue appear in the sky, glass-clear. The first summer days have arrived.

8 July
Setting off

By four o'clock it is already light. Emerging from the tent in the grey gloom, I feel light-hearted. It's time, for the air is fresh and invigorating. Gazing round at the mountains, the glaciers, listening to the snow crunch underfoot, I lose track of why I am here and what I want to do even.

Michl and I have got up rather later than we planned. Despite the forthcoming assault, we don't feel any especial excitement. Who knows whether we'll make it or not! A snowstorm could drive us back, even today.

Breakfast in Base Camp is much the same as usual. Ros Alí serves steaming tea. We eat linseed biscuits straight from the open tin. It is cold, and only a glimmer of light penetrates the blue tent.

I set off, and all disquiet falls from me, all anxious deliberation evaporates. (Reinhold Messner)

I do not make my first stop until I'm on a big boulder half a mile behind

After a good two weeks of route preparation up to a height of 7400 metres, and two recuperative days at Base Camp (4950 m), Messner and Dacher climb up to Camp I on 8 July (6100 m), to Camp II (6700 m) on the ninth, to Camp III (7350 m) on the tenth. On 11 July they climb to a height of 7910 m over terrain unknown to them, put up a bivouac tent there and from it the following day reach the summit. (Joachim Hoelzgen)

Base Camp on the flat glacier. The sun is just catching the summit of K2. It looks as if it were exploring it. The snow and ice flanks begin to come to life. The caress lasts several minutes. I feel a sudden surge of hope, and at the same time, completely lose all sense of scale. I no longer have the slightest idea how high this mountain is, how far it towers over me. My eyes are merely attracted to its summit. That, at least I know.

Michl didn't leave when I did. I can now see him coming, a little black dot on the dirty glacier.

'The light is extraordinarily clear today,' I say to him when he catches me up. I wonder if that is a good sign? This sun! Like a midsummer morning in the Western Alps.

As I climb on, I interrupt my rhythm from time to time to glance at the sunlit slopes. Now, too, the first rays of sun are washing over the mountains which border Base Camp to the west, and whose shapes have grown very familiar since we've been here. Clear and bright, they stand out diaphanously against the still, glassy background. Even the sky has a texture of space. Tattered banners of cloud cling around the summit, fluttering in the wind.

How harmonious it all is. Everything rhymes. I cease to think about myself, or even of this landscape. I go, merely, I look. That's where we want to be, up there! That is the only, the all-engulfing thought.

Slowly, and in a great arc, we turn right towards the start of the climb. Michl and I use the old route, climbing the snow slope to the right of the Abruzzi Spur. We never discussed it between us, why we should settle for this in preference to the usual approach. This is the way we went when we set up the first and second camps a good couple of weeks ago now, and again when we were up fixing ropes on the stretch to Camp III.

So now, we take our usual line, for the last time. In sharp zigzags we cover the ground, its surface crust roughened by the sun. I support myself lightly on my axe, so that my whole weight rests on the mountain-edge of my boot-sole, which at each step, I thrust deep into the firn. We each move at our own pace, uninfluenced by the other.

Nor in Camp I is there any hurry. We stretch out, doze, sleep, and now and again make some tea. We have to drink a lot.

9 July

Messner and Dacher climb from Camp I up to Camp II. At the same time Alessandro Gogna and Renato Casarotto move from Base to Camp I. Robert Schauer and Friedl Mutschlechner are to leave Base Camp the day following.
(Joachim Hoelzgen)

Elation in the morning at the sight of the sun! The valleys below are filled with haze. The slopes seem to steam. But towards the west it is clear. The view stretches so far that I make no attempt to count the peaks. Everytime I look up at the sky, I invariably take a couple of involuntary steps, despite my morning stiffness.

In the middle of Great Tower I stop. I want to rest and look around here halfway between Camps I and II. I sit for quite a while, alone. I look down at the ice rivers and moraines, which seem to stretch further the longer I stare at them. In huge meanders they flow down to Base Camp and beyond to Concordia where they discharge into the Baltoro Glacier in a sharp right hand bend. From above, these glaciers look like wide highways. Beyond them the mountain ranges are frosted over; in between the sinuous humps of moraine; the straight line of the horizon, from where we came.

The naked skeleton of the world, a building site which the Creator prematurely abandoned. (Charles Bruce)

Above the Baltoro Glacier the air seems to sway, to hover, an amorphous mass. We are already quite high, I think, and then, 'Suppose we do make it this time, that would be crazy!' Isn't it strange how transparent the air is here? I picture myself down there, walking up, K2 the Great Unknown ahead of me. What wonderful madness this climb is, and the possibility of looking down upon myself. I then think myself lucky when I consider the view from below.

The wind whistles among the rocks. But my thoughts keep winging back down to the valleys, to the rivers of ice. Again I see myself being lured towards the familiar thought: going back down, with the mountain behind me. That's something I know, that the beauty of mountaineering isn't in always going upwards. Upwards! That brings me back to my senses. I look up and want to go on.

I stand up with a jerk, hoist up my rucksack and take a few steps. Climbing is strenuous at this height. The steepness of the face, the smooth rocks on which my crampons can frequently find no grip, force me into an uneven rhythm. I climb round a corner, rest. The sun beats down heavily on my back like a second burden. It is several minutes before the strength seeps back into my legs and arms.

I always feel fine when I'm on the move, climbing; that applies mentally too. Even resting – at first with my lungs still gasping and my heart beating right into my throat – it's fine.

Afterwards in camp I begin to think over my fantasies of the day; I want to experience life mentally as well as physically, and that I don't manage. Inside the tent – the floor is scarcely as big as a single bed – we sit for a long while sorting out our gear. It is all very tight, but cosy. Michl says the same thing, so it's not just my imagination.

Security? That's not quite the feeling a 'nest' such as this evokes. It's a sort of security, true, but we are not bedded in here, just encapsulated and tucked away in the mountain. Pretty soon I forget where I am. Know only that self-made restrictions, the domestic, the safe, pay no dividends. I tuck myself up with the world.

I am no longer myself, and yet once again I am. (Reinhold Messner)

My thoughts don't concentrate on the dangers which surround us, nor on the rigours that await us, nor yet on the distances that separate us from the rest of mankind. Only that I am here. That at least is not difficult. I open up the tent and lean out to collect some snow. There's a pair of crampons lying on the stones, and nearby, an axe. Far below in the valley, the air shivers. Or does it just seem to me that it does?

Inside the tent, the purr of the stove; Michl rolling over in his sleeping bag. Cramped cosiness – and then, looking out again, this sheer endless drop. Stones, on which ice crystals glisten; the gentlest breath of wind bringing shivers to my face – what now is reality?

In the afternoon we sleep for a while. Then suddenly, as one, leap up. A falling stone thunders into our consciousness. There is no time to tear open the door of the tent. We can only hope that we are not in its path.

10 July

A Change in the Weather

On this, our third climbing day, the weather seems to change completely. The sun is still high in the sky, but it casts a pallid light, becoming eerie even as the day wears on. Mist collects in the valleys, blue or blue-green. The absence of wind is oppressive. The fact that we decide to continue is

The wonderful twilight enfolds me and fills me with freedom – also perhaps with longing and with sadness. It is as if a time awaited me, which has yet to come – the twilight over the valleys.
(Reinhold Messner)

more a matter of instinct, than the dictate of experience or intelligence. The fixed ropes make easy work of the Black Pyramid, the most difficult section on the Abruzzi Ridge; a stroll compared to the same climb a week ago. Camp III, which was put up by Friedl and Robert, is still standing. The snow slopes above look rather sinister though, as does the hazy sky and the build-up of cirrus formations over Sinkiang and Tibet. Now in the afternoon, all the weather signs still point to 'bad'. There is a transparent mist in the valleys, opalescent like milk-glass. Clouds are piling up in the west, and above them, layers of mist. The mountains appear both near and far away.

During the evening the outlook appears even worse, although during the night a sharp north wind drives away the cloud and dissolves the mist. But for this we would have abandoned our summit attempt.

All night long the storm chases around our tent. Michl and I, united in the worry that the tent will not stand up to the strain, are for hours on end each other's only hope. It is as if we were experiencing the end of the world, as if we were suspended, buffeted by the wind, in a universe beyond time and space. How it howls and whistles around the tent! Every pole, every thread has its own individual wail.

Shortly before waking, I dream that K2 vanishes forever, and us along with it; spirited away, as if it had never existed. But then, when I look outside, it is already light and the sky as clear and calm as I had seen it outspread in my dream of the void.

It is a flawless, clear, cool morning. Mist lingers only in the distant valleys. It looks as if the world was smothered behind it. Opposite us stands Broad Peak in all its glory. The high driven clouds between, make it seem to be constantly changing in size and shape. The moon, still visible on the western horizon, is nearly full.

11 July
Assault Camp

Today we must get away early. We want to finish cooking before the sun comes up. Before we went to bed Michl put a bag of snow at the bottom of our sleeping bags so that we shouldn't lose any time this morning brewing up our tea. As we set off, the sun reflects so brightly off the billowing snow slopes above, that it is hard to make out any crevasses. I prod the white wind-whipped surface cautiously with my axe. Step by step I test the way until we reach the edge of the blunt ridge separating the South and East Flanks. Here the snow is patchily hard. Michl catches me up. Sometimes we break through the surface of the pressed snow, disappearing up to our middles. Like moles we burrow in the mealy white stuff, leaving an open trench behind us.

We avoid a huge serac by making a right hand meander. Taking it in turns to lead, we toil up a steep snowfield, dangerously ready to avalanche, then I cut through the cornice and climb up onto the Shoulder. That's that done!

We take a rest. The extent of the gentle snow slopes rising above us is alarming. It looks like an eternity between us and the summit. The heat is not oppressive. We pull ourselves together. The loose snow, composed of blue-white crystals, lies ankle-deep on a hard undersurface. It crunches under our crampons at each step and the sound is a comforting one. Now, climbing slowly, comes a feeling of lightness, of having no distinct form

The endlessness of these domed snow slopes suggest eternity. And this eternity is such that it permits us to pass to the summit.
(Reinhold Messner)

as I move over this wide whaleback of snow. Tiredness. No sense of gravity left in me at all, just lungs and a heart which keeps forcing the chest ever wider. I am no longer corporate, but a floating surface, not unlike the surface on which I stand, walk. Walk – stand – walk.

Reaching a flat spot between the Shoulder and the Bottleneck, I throw off my rucksack. I want to check how high we are already; 7950 metres according to the altimeter. That may well be right. Then again, it seems too much to me, and I put the instrument away – that's my old fear, of deceiving myself at this altitude.

The wind blows the snow over the ridge. The sun now stands high and the sky is so black that one thinks it must be dark behind it. At altitude all fine weather days are the same.

'Beautiful spot,' says Michl.

'Mmm, yes,' I answer.

'We'll be out of the wind, over to the left.'

'True.'

I look at Michl squatting in front of me and in so doing notice the frosty sun, surrounded by an aureole in which snow crystals dance.
(Reinhold Messner)

'We'll need to dig the tent in,' says Michl.

'Oh, no, I don't think that will be necessary,' I reply.

Our tent is red and blue. Further down we used green and yellow ones, or just blue. And in Base Camp the tents are red.

At this height camps are only safe if the tent can be tucked in under an overhang. Then it can't be harmed by either rock or ice. But here there are no overhangs, and thus, no ideal bivouac sites. We look for the best we can find. It is a niche, which we stamp out in the 30 degrees of slope of firm snow and ice. We anchor the tent with axes and pegs. It is tucked in between waist-high snowdrifts and a flattened ridge on the right hand side. It will offer shelter from any storms blowing in from Sinkiang. Looking at it, it reminds you of the hatchway at the top of a ski jump; this jump falls steeply away for 3000 metres right down to the Godwin-Austen Glacier at the foot of K2.

I had actually hoped to climb up as far as the final bivouac site used by the Italians, but realised as we went on that this was too far. Michl agreed, 'It's better here.' All the same, I know that's not really true. The higher we get today, the less we have to climb tomorrow. And who knows what the snow is like higher up.

The summit pyramid showing the bivouac spot.

Michl is optimistic. 'Six hours should be enough to polish off this dome,' he says, convinced that we will get to the summit tomorrow. But there is still a long night ahead of us, a night in the death zone. And it's nights like these that scare me; I'm like a child in a dark cellar.

Dusk comes slowly as if the night were being still further protracted for us. Cold seeps up through the thin foam-rubber mats, bringing agony with it. I feel as if isolated sensations, each sharply detached, are tearing me from the mountain; as if doubts about my oneness were again creeping up on me. It is not the physical effort, not the heat or the cold, which so often drive me to despair, but this terror which takes a hold of me during inactivity, and against which there is no antidote.

I am convinced that Michl underestimates how much we still have to do to reach the summit. I cannot share his optimism. And I cannot shake off the misgivings, which, with increasing darkness, turn to fear. But it is not the wild, confused, agitation of panic, I feel, but rather the gentle gnawing

Besides all the predictable circumstances on high mountains, there are also the unpredictable. Only because I place myself and K2 beyond predictabilities, do we grow into what we really are.
(Reinhold Messner)

of a thousand doubts, and it sweeps over me whenever I'm only half awake, tormenting, disturbing me.
Michl brings in snow for the last time, snow which he leaves before melting, until he has warmed his hands inside his sleeping bag. Carefully he zips up the entrance again and stuffs his empty sleeping bag cover into the tiny gap in the right hand corner where the two zips meet. So, now, we are moderately protected from the full force of the storm.
Cooking at this altitude is a strenuous and tedious business. We take it in turns. First one, then the other keeps hold of the little pan. It takes an hour before the meal is ready: soup, warm tuna fish, a wedge of bread, followed by tea.
In the light of the gas flame Michl's face looks tight with strain, a look of concentration as if he were constantly trying to do something better, or understand a problem exactly. His voice has got slower, too, and his movements deliberate. We don't talk much. Now and then Michl will mutter something, but as if he only wanted to say something to himself.
For a while we just lie moaning, waiting – without really knowing for what. Although we're both thirsty, we can't seem to rouse ourselves to do anything about preparing a drink. I think of nothing in particular. Quite absurd things run through my head. Occasionally I drop off to sleep. But the knowledge that we really have to drink something keeps dragging me back to consciousness.
Michl, too, is awake. Our breath where it touches the tent, condenses, turns to hoar frost, then trickles back onto our faces in crystalline form.

12 July
Summit Climb

There are moments when you ask yourself, 'What am I doing here? Why aren't I lying at home in my warm bed? (Michl Dacher)

I wake at two, and prod Michl through his layers of sleeping bag, down suit, silk underclothing.
'Michl, we must start cooking!' He only groans, later comes his 'Yeah.'
Yet even as he leans outside the tent to fill his bag with more snow, in temperatures of minus 30, I have already dropped off to sleep again. And no sooner do I take over and melt snow than Michl dozes off again. It takes hours before we have a drink ready.
We only wake up properly after tea and hot soup. And then to crown it all, towards morning a storm sweeps in from China, blowing in the walls of the tent at our back. We wanted to set off while it was still dark, but the storm pins us fast inside the tent.
'This is tough luck,' I say.
'We'll be up in six hours,' Michl is confident.
The sun comes up shortly after five, streaming bright and warm through the blue nylon. But we still can't go outside, even though it's more important than anything to be on top in good time so that we can get back to the tent before night sets in.
Finally, at seven o'clock, the wind dies down. As we crawl outside, the harsh sunlight makes us blink. We are both wearing our blue, down filled suits, facing each other like men from the moon. I think, I must look as odd as Michl does, all muffled up. His movements are ponderous, as if in slow motion; his face looks small and pointed.
While I'm putting on my crampons, he ducks back inside the tent. Then he goes halfway round the outside, then back inside again, as if he had mislaid something important. Then he starts busying himself with his

Himalayan climbing is not necessarily the ultimate expression of the art. In other parts of the world, the style of an ascent means more than the attainment of a summit. By their nature, Himalayan peaks inhibit the style of a climb. (Galen Rowell)

Michl finds a ledge which he extends by cutting steps in the ice with his axe. This way the men are able to traverse left out of the barrier and onto a snow slope. (Joachim Hoelzgen)

crampons. Meanwhile I pick up my axe, take a couple of steps, stop, move another few paces.
Over my shoulder I smile back at Michl, 'Everything alright?'
'Oh, fine. Very good in fact.'
'Okay,' I call, and, 'Don't forget to do up the tent.'
Resolutely I set off. A short way above, on the ridge, I stop, and with a tilt of my head, enquire of Michl whether I should wait for him. But he signals that it is not necessary. He puts something inside, pulls up the zipper and seals the tent.
Soon he is no more than a dark spot. The snow is still so hard that only the tips of the crampons leave any mark on it. The steep, exposed snow slope presents no problems. All the same I hold my axe in my right hand, at the ready, just for balance. I traverse out left, stopping to rest where the wall drops sheer and steep below me, right down to Base Camp, before I double back across the ridge again. It must have been somewhere here that Walter Bonatti and his Hunza porter bivouacked when they brought up oxygen supplies for the summit pair, Compagnoni and Lacedelli, during the first ascent in 1954.
Continuing to zig-zag, I head for the cleft which cuts clean through the entire width of the cliff above me, as if sliced with a knife. An avalanche must have come down from there some days before, a slab avalanche – 80 centimetres thick and half a square kilometre in size. This will be a critical passage, I know. If the snow above is hard, we're alright. But if it's soft and deep, as the cutaway indicates, then we have no chance at all. These thoughts occupy me as I climb up, briefly on the rocks, and then back left onto the open slope of the great basin which, further up, narrows into the Bottleneck. Meanwhile, I don't let myself look up. Things go more quickly, I know, if I don't keep looking to see how far it is.
Above the notch, I thrust my axe into the snow. And stop, stricken, it is like accumulated quicksand. That's that then – hopeless! I gasp for breath, everything is whirling and my body feels like lead. I don't know why I don't turn back at once. I don't even look back towards Michl. In a fit of defiance, I pull out my axe and wade on through the snow. I can't and won't believe this is how it is – snow drifts waist-deep.
I trample it down and plough across to the rocks on the left, but they, too, offer no salvation. Bottomless powder snow covers everything. I consider whether it wouldn't be more sensible to climb the rocks immediately above me. That way I could avoid the effort, and eliminate the danger which increases with every step in this avalanche gully. But the rocks are too steep, to say nothing of being glazed with ice. Besides, we have no rope.
Michl quickly catches me up. Having lost my original climbing rhythm by the heavy work of breaking trail, I make further progress only in fits and starts. A few steps – rest – another few steps. The Bottleneck, that narrow snow couloir between two ridges of rock beneath the giant ice cliffs, is steeper than I had thought looking at it from below. And here, too, the snow is deep and fathomless. It is not strength of will that propels me forward, it is force of habit. As if to climb higher was part of my destiny: this old quest after harmony and synthesis; this hunger for perfection and fulfilment – produce a driving force against all rational

considerations!
Above the Bottleneck, where the snow gives way to the vertical ice of the summit seracs, I start to traverse out left. I suppose that there will be a point of weakness where the rocks join the overhanging ice. But far from it. The ice is brittle and crumbles away at each stroke of the axe. The axe won't grip. I am too weak to cut holds. So I retreat.

At 12.40 Reinhold Messner advises Base Camp over his walkie-talkie that he is 'in snow up to my arse.' His altimeter reads 8350 metres. 'You think you're almost at the summit once you're over the barrier, but with every step the way gets longer,' he says between gasps.
(Joachim Hoelzgen)

Meanwhile, Michl is below me and tries to climb the rocks to the left. He balances, dextrously, across two little outcrops of rock. That is going to be too dangerous as well. So I reach my axe over towards him and he catches hold of the shaft and pulls himself up beside me. We weigh up the possibilities. Then Michl continues the traverse. Feet on the rocks, hands in the snow, he burrows his way a dozen paces to the left. Then he meets blank ice, but it's only two steps wide before again it's deep powder snow. We take it in turns to work our way through it.
After this section we come out onto a slope, again covered with deep, soft, snow – a legacy of the massive amounts of new snow that fell in the North Pakistan mountains this spring. Like two sausage dogs in deep snow, we have to burrow our way up the slope. For a while we worry that the mass of snow will come away and carry us with it down to the Godwin-Austen Glacier. If this were the Alps, we would have turned back. It is already mid-day before we reach the rock boulder that lies marooned, in the snowfield to the left of the great seracs. Snow, snow, snow . . . as far as the eyes can see. And above, the blue-black sky.
Our progress has become an uneven crawl. The snow slope ahead stretches out endlessly. I don't want to believe it: with every metre we force ourselves upwards, the slope stretches further. All this untrodden emptiness robs me of any sense of distance. I never once see our tracks on the slope beneath us. They are lost. Endlessly, eternally, we climb through the snow. Why do I keep climbing if I know we shall never reach the summit? The sun is on its way down and it is already ice cold.
We do still have some time left, although to me it seems we are much too late for the summit. This continual feeling of helplessness everytime I take a rest and then look up to see how far we still have to go. It doesn't occur to me that dimensions can be very distorted at great heights.
The snow slope ahead of me is not desolate, just in a strange way, never-ending. Where the wind has fashioned the snow into strange sculptings, the shadows are darker. All around, the same colour, the colour of shadows. The sky is grey-blue, and the snow too wears the colour of the sky. Only high above does the world still shine with colour. Somewhere there is the way to deliverance. In some places the edges of the wind formations are so thin and transparent that I dare not touch them. I don't want to destroy their delicate perfection. But once my gloved fingers have broken them, I think no more about my following crampons. When I move, it is the movement of an animal; when I rest, I am a rock. The responsibility for our continued existence is no longer mine alone to bear. I think Michl will let me know if he wants to go back. I'm only worried about his hands. So long as Michl says nothing, then I want to go on. I think this looking back at him. His movements are those of a drunk, yet at the same time they are purposeful and obviously directed upwards. There still seems to be no end to this slope. I become worried. Since we are

What this mountain has to offer, is the more killing and depressing, because all you really feel like is some wretched little earwig scrabbling to get out of a bathtub.
(Michl Dacher)

At 15.00 hours Reinhold comes on again. Altimeter reading: 8460 metres, snow increasingly deep, 'One slope after the other . . . we are very tired although we are taking it in turns to break trail.' Later Messner says, 'It was like floundering in an uphill swamp.' (Joachim Hoelzgen)

climbing in shadow, it is impossible to gauge the exact position of the sun. Silently we wallow our way through the snow. Michl in front, I behind, or the other way about. I am proud of each metre we gain. We leave a perfect trail, yet it is not without danger. In places it is as steep as a church roof, and below us, further down, the wall drops away vertically. I know that were one of us to slip, we should have no hope of survival.

Then the slope eases off and becomes at the same time, less hazardous. Our gloves are encased in an armour of snow. Our feet are clumps, made up of boot, gaiters and ice. We look like lost polar explorers. We continue working steadily and thanklessly. When one of us takes a rest, the other doesn't stare at him.

'Put your down gloves on,' I say to Michl, as he catches me up. The air is now bitterly cold. Michl informs me he hasn't got any down gloves; he has left them behind.

Burrowing our way forward, we are like marathon runners reaching the end of their strength without knowing how far it still is to the finish.

Again, I advance a fair distance, but when I look back I can't make out where it was I last rested. It seems so far. Michl goes ahead to forge the way, stamping snow, wading. Far below in the open snowfield, there is a kind of fissure, otherwise there is no shelter in any direction. By a wind-fashioned pinnacle, I take a rest, leaning on my axe. I hunch up with weariness, without first stamping out a platform in the snow.

I can hear a rumbling from within the snow. It is so near that I brace myself to hang on tightly before I realise what it is. Then comes the sound of crampons above me, Michl is crawling on all fours. You can even swim in this snow – swim upwards. I'm getting cold standing about, I must move on. Michl waits so that I can take over the lead. Passing him, I fancy I don't know his face. We'll never manage the rest of the way if we continue crawling.

The distances we put between one rest and the next get shorter all the time. Only, I don't know how long they are. I can't count the steps as I go along, and resting, I can't fix my mind on anything. Then, when I set myself in motion again, everything in me is involved, mental as well as physical. This hasn't got much to do with climbing any more. It's more a matter of endurance, holding out, suffering a torture beyond pain and exhaustion. We only keep going because each one of us hopes the other will give in first. It has become a dogged struggle with each other. And Michl, who is a tough 45 year old, is, when it comes to giving up first, as stubborn as I.

On the summit pyramid the snow gradually diminishes. The ridge ahead of me runs crescent-wise to the left, easy to climb, but unbearably long. I can't estimate its distance. 'My strength isn't going to last out!' In places the snow is now quite hard. So I make faster progress without being consciously aware of it. Suddenly, I'm standing in the sun, and know at once that we are on the summit.

'We're there, we're on top!'

My exclamation has apparently shaken Michl out of some sort of trance, he looks at me with such a startled expression. Standing here on the line between light and shadow, I can at last get my bearings. The ridge now looks quite short. Below, right, a rock boulder. In front of me a cornice which overhangs out to the left, the south. So, I must therefore be on the

At 16.40 Messner advises Base Camp: 'Summit reached . . . we are okay . . . no hallucinations, no emotional outbursts. Merely thankfulness for the marvellous fact that we don't need to climb any higher.'
(Joachim Hoelzgen)

The summit is not important, but it is that point where I can most easily give expression to my energy. I can achieve a mental balance that I do not feel if I fail to reach the top. . . . When I'm able to express all my energy, to lodge it all on a single point, it comes back to me, again, transformed.
(Alessandro Gogna)

north side, the sunny side. In no time at all I am warm.
'We're up!' Again I yell the words to Michl. I want to give him my hand, though he is still ten steps away. I wait. Then we meet. I toss off my rucksack. For a while we can only stand there, unable to believe it. We are surprised, and forget the reason for being here. It is a very fine thing to stand thus and look closely into your inmost self.
Michl's face wears again the cheeky expression that he had at the outset. We communicate without words. I keep quiet, just listen, watching his movements and what he says with his eyes. Again, it is him who comes to himself first. Like him I want to share our good news. Eventually, I remember the radio, pull it out of the rucksack, and switch it on; 'Kappa Due to Base Camp, Kappa Due to Base Camp, please come in.' The reception is poor, but good enough to give our position and hear the congratulations and delight of Joachim in Base Camp.
I pass the apparatus over to Michl, he squats down, and as I plod up to the highest bump on the ridgetop, I hear him ordering flowers for his wife. The exhaustion, which only a few moments ago I could hardly contain, now on the summit feels like serenity. A peace that is compounded of strength and self-possession. Despite the many doubts about this climb, it could not have turned out differently. Had I not reached the summit, I would have disintegrated – like a mountain, into many stones.
The view is clear in all directions, for nearly 200 miles. An air of happiness hangs over everything. This is the most beautiful panorama I have ever seen! Only in the east does the shadow of K2, like a great black wedge, grip the highlands of Sinkiang. Its sharp outline lies across the earth like a tomb.
For a short while I take off my gloves to make it easier to work the camera and radio. Whenever I touch the snow, my fingers turn white and I rub them on the legs of my trousers, stuffing them in my pockets in between times.
I look for a recognisable clue on the mountain's shadow, and find it in the shape of a tiny dash, like a pencil, on the summit far below. That has to be me. This makes me laugh. Such a strange feeling to see one's own shadow cast for miles onto the earth. It reminds me of death. Now I know where I come from and where I'm going.
I turn round to look at the sun sinking over the western horizon. A scene virtually unchanged for thousands of years. You can tell that from the colours. Where there are no settlements, the blue above the valleys is more tranquil, more serene. To the north over Sinkiang, the world seems more sombre and disturbed. Mountains and valleys blur together in the shadows. But as my glance rests briefly on the steep granite towers of the Ogre and Latok, and onto Concordia where the great glaciers flow together like some motorway junction, taking in Broad Peak as well, these mountains then seem to emerge out of their shadows, whilst the valleys become invisible. The horizon leaps. It seems as if the world stops behind it.
Looking away from the western horizon, my gaze again concentrates on the summits. This time round I identify the mountains and valleys of this the most peaceful spot on earth.
A little while later I stow the camera and radio back into my rucksack.

Michl and I start off eastwards along the ridge. We are still in the sunshine. Then we drop off the ridge to the south-east side. Night enfolds us. In an instant it becomes bitterly cold.

As we stop in front of a narrow crevasse, I point to Michl's nose. It is almost white. His beard is a fringe of ice.

'You look like a polar explorer,' I tell him.

'You don't look much different yourself,' he replies, and as he speaks, he cracks the layer of ice over his face. With long, heavy steps we lunge downwards through the snowfield. There is avalanche danger, but it doesn't particularly bother me. Sometimes I make out a crevasse. The snow is slightly darker if there is one lurking below it. Jumping across, I warn Michl. The long chain of snowdrifts, which we pass with great care so as not to suddenly find ourselves disappearing into bottomless snow, are also darker than the light, rolling, even snow slopes. But just where it looks harmless, I pay particular attention.

I can still hear Michl's footsteps although he has dropped far behind me. And though I am headed downwards, I still 'see' his cheerful face. Looking round periodically to satisfy myself he's alright, what I see is a younger man, like a drunk dancing in his movements. How beautiful, how happy he is. And from the summit, he ordered flowers for his wife!

The air whispers around me and the first star appears in the sky. I look down over the shadowy ridges which stretch from the foot of K2 for hundreds of miles to north and east. The world down there, cool and aloof, both tempts and repels me at one and the same time; as does, even more so, the shadow of K2, which grows longer by the minute and upon which I seem to be standing. I look again at my feet wading through the snow. Slowly I am making my way back to the world, a world to which I no longer belong.

My face is numb with cold by the time I collapse face down in the snow in front of the bivouac tent. All my bones ache. Nothing to drink. For a long time I sit fiddling with my gaiters. I can't undo them. I can only get my crampons off my boots. My gloves are torn to pieces, feathers in the snow. I look round and see that Michl is no longer that far away. A black, swaying, elongated dot, he approaches over the ridge between the south and east flanks, in a direct line for the tent.

The descent has only taken two hours. How was that possible?

'Traversing across to the Bottleneck wasn't so difficult,' says Michl.

'No, that's what I thought,' I answer, carefully plucking the icicles from the hairs of my beard.

We have trampled out a foot-wide clearway round our tent, and there I dump my crampons. Michl stands in front of me grinning. He, too, is encrusted in ice.

At that moment the shadow of K2 has reached its longest. On its summit the small spot can still be seen. And still I have the feeling that this little projection is me, my other non-tangible self. Nor am I really mistaken. It indicates the direction I have to go. The vision lingers for a moment. Then I crawl into the tent.

There is a lumpy heap between the two sleeping mats; I almost fall over it as I crawl in. I fidget about, trying to get comfortable; it's all uneven and hard. There must be something underneath the mattress, but I can't find

K2 from the east, showing the bivouac under the summit pyramid; in profile below the Shoulder, the Abruzzi Ridge.

The result, the reaching of a summit, is of minor importance; but the pleasure, the discipline, the whole merit of the climb, depend upon the way it was done, that is the method, behavior and mental attitude of the climbers during the ascent, the descent, and the whole long day. The result of a climb is negligible, the satisfaction in it soon passes; but the process is vitally important, because its human effect will be lasting.
(Geoffrey Winthrop Young)

anything. I try and decide what we can eat tonight, but I'm not successful in that either.
My sleeping bag is still lying in the middle of the tent where I left it. Absentmindedly I start shoving mats and bits and pieces of clothing around. Then I begin unpacking my rucksack, but abandon it halfway through. A bit later I fiddle with the knobs of the radio, unable to decide whether or not to switch it on. Finally, I spread out my sleeping bag on the mattress and crawl inside.
We are both too tired to cook, or even to sleep. The blue colour of the tent diffuses the starlight. In the half-dark I see ice crystals glistening on the fabric. How strange everything looks at night. How strange I seem too, in my exhaustion. Half-lifting myself up in an endeavour to find a new comfortable position, I look across at Michl. He, too, is lying there desperately. The whole night is one of utter fatigue, tossing and moaning by turn, muffled in our sleeping bags. Every bone aches. Soon the cold penetrates both tent and down. I touch myself lightly in the way one might out of habit reach for one's partner, as if I could warm myself thereby. It is of no special significance, a reflex action merely. In sleep, some part of me often stays awake waiting for someone some part that makes life bearable and confirms my reality.

13 July
Descent through Blizzard

With deep longing I think of a possible world in which this safety and security were possible without all the effort; in which a sense of belonging were also possible, unfettered by degrees of altitude, primitive landscape, sicknesses and doubt.
(Reinhold Messner)

I wake up at three; there's another storm outside. I imagine myself outside, face into the wind. Already my thoughts are whirling in concert with the whirling of the powder snow around the tent, until an abrupt lull in the wind puts an end to them. Faced with the prospect of sheer loneliness, I try and bury myself in the mountain completely. That for me is the only salvation in these fitful hours between waking and sleeping, hours of heightened realisation. Only folded in the arms of the world do I feel safe, secure.
Eventually I say, 'We've got to cook something.'
'Yeah,' Michl replies and immediately closes his eyes again.
Later he fetches in some snow and we make two cups of tea. We're still too tired to cook. Towards morning we toss sleeplessly on the thin, hard, mat, backwards and forwards. We won't leave until the tent is warm. The ski sticks I left sticking in the snow outside the tent a couple of days ago, are still there. I hang my ice-covered gaiters on them so that they flutter like flags in the wind. They will be a landmark for the next party.
Patches of cloud and powder snow spill in from the west, over the ridge and past the tent. It is as if a curtain of vapour hangs in front of the sun. Only in the north-east is the air still calm and clear.
The tent throws an over-large shadow onto the snow. To me now, everything seems very simple and obvious. We have plenty of time for the descent, we can take frequent rests. Our weariness makes us like sleep-walkers, and many things look quite different from before. Not just as if I had never been here before, but as if nobody had.
Suddenly at one and the same time we have cloud, darkness, drifting snow and blizzard. It all happens in an instant, directly overhead, so quickly that we lose all sense of direction. Propped on our crampons we crouch on the ice and let the worst pass over. But we won't make any progress like this. There's only a brief respite, the sun comes out for one short minute,

We have done everything possible, and have given a meaning to the nonsense of our being here. That is the impression imparted by one last, short look back at the summit. (Reinhold Messner)

then hailstones start leaping down the ice-slopes at us, accompanied by more chasing banks of cloud.

We cautiously make our way down from one ice bulge to the next. We have practically no idea which way we should be going. Ironic to have got to the top and then die on the way down. Too late now for regrets. Sheltering for a few moments in a hollow, I ask myself, 'To climb K2, what sense is there in that?'

The frightful bombardment starts up again just behind the South Shoulder. The mist grows thicker. Snowdrifts pile up, intermingled with hailstones. The black cloud holds no promise of improvement this morning, just more of the same. Bleak prospect. Fumbling in near darkness, we seek shelter under the huge serac. Sit down and wait till it eases a bit.

Lumps of snow roll down towards us. Two blurred figures emerge through the mist. Even at a distance of two metres, we cannot distinguish which is Messner and which Dacher. (Friedl Mutschlechner)

A bit further on we huddle down again. Staring for a moment into the seething, simmering clouds, I grow quite dizzy. Jagged clouds, ever darker, whistle past us, sometimes blotting each other from view. With all this going, stopping, peering, doubt, I imagine myself to be a patch of cloud.

Suddenly we make out three shadowy shapes far below us – and immediately feel a wave of the utmost relief. It is Sandro, Friedl and Robert climbing up to the last camp. It can't be much further, then, to the third camp now.

'We must take care not to walk right past them in the mist,' I say to Michl.

'No,' he replies, 'better to wait for them.'

'Oh, no,' I say, 'we'll keep going down slowly, but not too far.' Half an hour later we're standing facing each other. We get a warm reception, and call a short halt in Camp III. Sandro makes some tea. Michl grows jolly as he drinks. He holds his mug of drink like a key in both hands. Between sips he plucks at his ice-encrusted beard.

On Friday, 13 July, the trio from Camp III (7350 m) head over the long snow slope towards the bivouac at 7910 metres, where Messner and Dacher spent the nights before and after their summit climb. (Joachim Hoelzgen)

There follows a discussion: Friedl is all in favour of the three of them waiting in Camp III for better weather, but Robert opposes him. It would be decidedly more sensible, he argues, to go back down to Base and wait there for the weather to improve. 'In Camp III we would deteriorate physically if we spent many days here. And besides that we would consume provisions we might urgently need if we were to get pinned down on the mountain by a storm!'

I say, 'You are responsible for yourselves. You must make up your own minds.' Robert, although he's only 25 years old, has already climbed three eight-thousanders. His experience gives the others qualms about contradicting him. Friedl hasn't been to the Himalaya before at all. It's Alessandro who has the casting vote, and he sides with the voice of experience.

The three follow Messner and Dacher back down to Base Camp. In so doing they relinquish their only chance at the summit, as it proves. By the fourteenth the weather is better and stays fine until the seventeenth. It would have been sufficient for a summit attempt from Camp III and a safe retreat. (Joachim Hoelzgen)

The wind is howling as we climb down over the Black Pyramid. There is nowhere to shelter. The rocks are precipitous, and when there is a narrow ledge, we find snow on it. Grey clouds continue to chase overhead, the rope is coated with a fuzz of new snow and the rocks in places with a layer of verglas. When the cloud does part for a little while, the drop below seems endless.

I am climbing down in the middle of the party. I can only pick out the person in front occasionally as a shadow between the clouds. There must

Only Robert in his enthusiasm is not saying what he really thinks. A young man of ambition, he is really envious of our summit climb. A hero more to himself than to others, pursued by an illusion of greatness he doesn't possess. (Reinhold Messner, diary)

be someone else not far behind as I can hear the scraping of his crampons, and now and again am pelted by lumps of snow. At intervals a blurred figure will loom out of the mist.

The tents, the glacier, the fixed rope – everything has changed since we climbed up. Even the people coming down with me, they too have changed. Michl is happy. Sandro and Friedl are pleased for us. I can read it in their eyes, but Robert's face wears a wry expression. He takes it hard that Michl and I have been to the top. Well I'm sorry. Envy can be a corrosive sickness.

Just above Camp II, it suddenly becomes light. The sun is not shining, it's true, but you can now see right down into Base Camp. Going along, with an eye to the grey sky, my steps drag without my being aware of it. The country below with its stumpy, grey mountains looks desolate, worn to its bare bones. Between the grey-white flanks of the mountain ranges, the river of ice flows wide and slow, its surface etched with the white bones of a giant saurian. 'K2', I say, to myself only.

The gulf separating the Matterhorn and K2 is less than the distance which separates the different sides of me. (Reinhold Messner)

The sun breaks through as in the evening we walk over the glacier and into Base Camp. Terry and Jochen come out to meet me. As I skirt the foot of K2 and look upwards, I see only vast, empty snowfields, and above them, nothing. A few ravens croak away overhead.

Climb to the Summit

Right: From the Godwin–Austen Glacier to the Shoulder of K2 is 2000 vertical metres of ice and rock. The team equips this stretch of the climb with two bivouac camps and fixed ropes. Remnants of ropes, ladders and bits and pieces of equipment still remain from earlier expeditions. Some material has been on the ridge since 1938, during which time it has rotted away under the ice.

I look over all the summits and valleys, 'Here I am,' says a voice inside me; I look and I see. But here, around me there is nothing of sense or of practical purpose; and so I stop altogether being that person who I had told myself I was.
(Reinhold Messner)

Below: There are no routes on the West Face of K2. An American team attempted a climb from the Savoia Pass in 1975, but failed (||||||||||). In 1978 an English expedition attacked the West Ridge (. . . . .). Both parties who had their sights set on the South Spur in 1979 were unable to realise their plans: the Messner expedition didn't even attempt it, and the French expedition foundered between the 'Mushroom' and the summit (– – –).
The South Face of K2 appeared to Reinhold Messner to offer a possibility, but he decided against it on account of avalanche danger (–·–·–·) after a reconnaissance thrust to mid-height.
The Abruzzi Ridge or Rib (— — —) has been scaled three times (1954 Italian, 1977 Japanese, 1979 Messner Expedition).

As a boy I had been excited by the first sight of the Alps. They were great enough. But this was greater far. I cannot remember having been struck with my own insignificance in comparison with this giant of a mountain. My dominant feeling was one of delight – of joy at having had the chance of seeing so wonderful a sight. And on that occasion, as well as two years later, when I traversed that marvellous region round K2, and, from close under them, saw its satellites of 27,000 feet, 26,000 feet, and 25,000 feet peaks, I feasted my soul on their beauty. But, full of spirit as I was, the idea that I, or anyone else, should presume to think of climbing any one of them never entered my mind. I believed myself adventurous, but adventurous to that extent I decidedly was not. My spirit was still at the pass level. It had risen above the valleys. But most certainly it had not risen to the peaks. When, therefore, I looked upon these giants round me, I just took it for granted that their summits were for ever beyond the reach of man.
(Sir Francis Younghusband)

Fortune is the fate I have chosen for myself. (Alessandro Gogna)

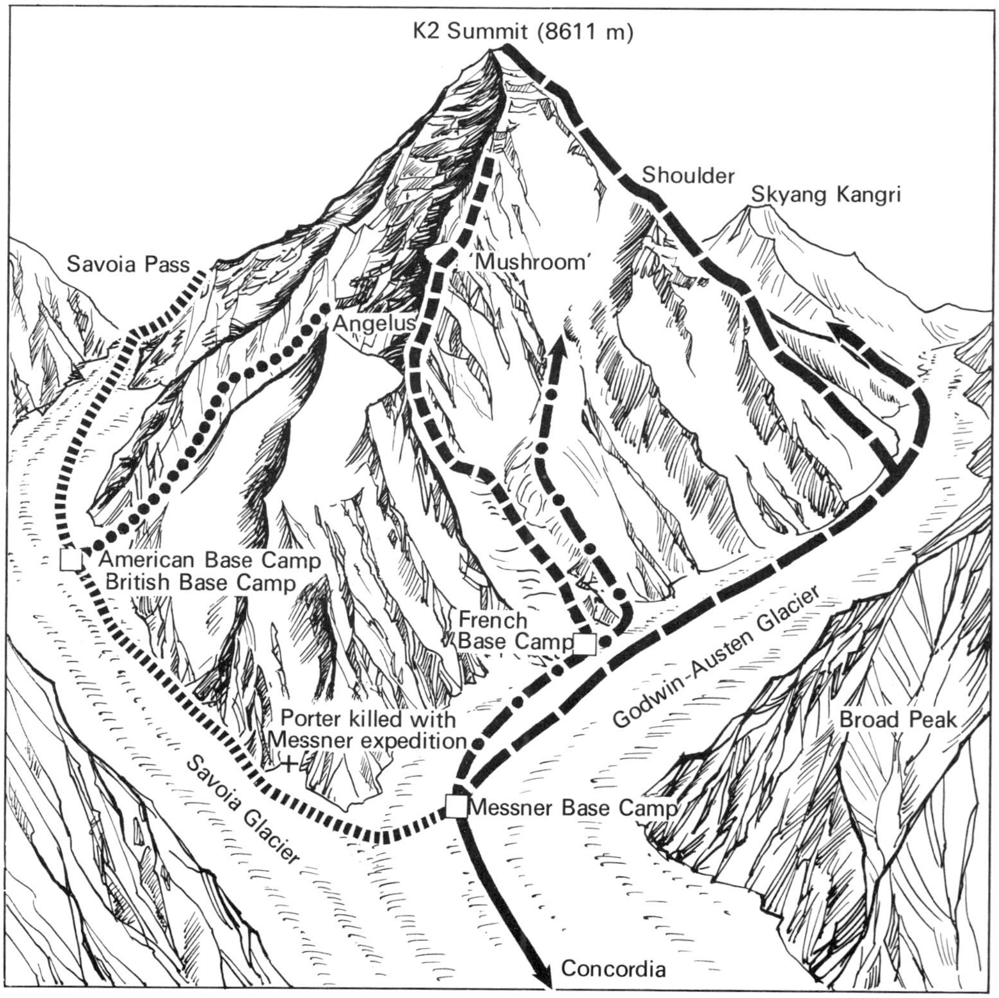

On a preliminary reconnaissance of the South Face of K2, Reinhold Messner and Friedl Mutschlechner manage to climb to over 6000 metres after a bivouac. However, seracs in the centre of the face force them to turn back, and eventually abandon the idea of scaling the South Face.

The climbing becomes more strenuous all the time, and often I find myself stuck waist-deep in the snow without really caring what happens to me – it is almost as if my judgment, my memory no longer exist. Then

as I labour for breath my will returns and drives me on – and on. But I don't know where this willpower comes from.
(Reinhold Messner)

Next double page: The way to the foot of the steep Abruzzi Rib leads over flat snowslopes and up a step in the Godwin-Austen Glacier between Broad Peak and K2, about two hours on foot. This section is under constant avalanche-threat, from left and right, and not infrequently the avalanches spill across the valley basin.

The team members have to continually find new ways through the ice pinnacles and crevasses to the start of the climb.

The Abruzzi Rib – eroded and sculpted by its bitter, changeable weather – in profile a steep/ even ridge – forms the ideal climbing route.
(Reinhold Messner)

The climb to Camp I at 6100 metres. In the tent (top to bottom): Friedl Mutschlechner, Michl Dacher, and Robert Schauer.

We lived in the little tent as if in a cave. It was never really gloomy and on its walls the scudding clouds cast their shadows.
(Reinhold Messner)

To keep the way to the Shoulder open, it has to be climbed repeatedly. The onset of bad weather while doing so forces the climber back to Base Camp.

In moments of enlightenment, I know – without the need of a God to tell me, what is beautiful and good.
(Reinhold Messner)

Poised between light and shadow – in House's Chimney – I feel completely whole again; for the first time since early morning, I am reminded of my own existence.
(Reinhold Messner)

In critical situations it is the person leading who solves the problem. A boss, as such, with supreme control, we don't have.
(Reinhold Messner)

At the start there is a quantity of snow and ice plugging the steep House's Chimney; later it gets easier to negotiate. Even so it is very wearisome bringing heavy loads up through it. The team are carrying all the equipment themselves. We are full of admiration for the American Expedition led by Charles Houston who solved this key passage way back in 1938. All later expeditions to the Abruzzi Rib have profited from their pioneer work. In 1954 the Italians built a rope-way through this section – as did Houston's expedition before them.

Camp II at 6700 metres. A few torn tents on the same spot are reminders of the Japanese expedition of 1977. Whenever a storm blows up the Messner team are forced to climb down as far as Base Camp, which is no longer distinguishable from this height.

What drives me to mountaineering, above all to rock climbing, is the need to be active and from time to time to push myself to utter physical and mental exhaustion – as well as the challenge of the new and the unknown.
(Renato Casarotto)

The climb to Camp III at 7350 metres. Technically this stretch is the most difficult.

This great spaciousness! In my relief and exhaustion, whole vastnesses fuse together – those newly-achieved and those experienced earlier – into an all-embracing world.
(Reinhold Messner)

MESSNER

The route between Camp III and the bivouac at about 8000 metres is very strenuous. The picture left shows the Gasherbrums, Broad Peak, and Chogolisa. After a night in the tent, on 12 July Reinhold Messner and Michl Dacher climb up through the 'Bottleneck' below the great summit cornice, then out to the left across steep, wide snowslopes to the summit.

At the hundredth rest – not far beneath the summit – the landscape grows distorted beneath us: the finely detailed summit crest to the south flattens out to a stumpy ridge; the meandering glacier beneath us appears as a single, black trench; and the growing shadow of K2 smothers all the mountains and valleys to the east.
(Reinhold Messner)

We cling to such extreme moments, in which we seem to die, yet are reborn.
(Peter Matthiessen)

Passing through the 'Bottleneck' precarious seracs threaten Messner and Dacher. They traverse away left from under these and struggle up through the deep snows of the summit dome.

The climbers kept in radio contact with Base Camp during their climb. From this height Concordia looks like a motorway intersection.

In such moments of supreme effort, my own death seems at the same time quite near yet quite impossible. Between vacillating moments of luck and indecision, I am aware that I tread the frontier of my own existence, which widens out before me beyond time and into space.
(Reinhold Messner)

Reinhold Messner on the summit of K2. The view is unsurpassably clear. To the south all the great Karakorum peaks (below left): Hidden Peak, Gasherbrums II, III, IV and the three mighty summits of Broad Peak. To the east a view over the russet-grey ranges of Sinkiang (above).

Suddenly, no will, no doubt, no more yearning, just an animal-like acceptance, an all-embracing feeling flowing through the whole body. (Reinhold Messner)

The shadow cast by K2 grows longer and longer, as does Michl Dacher's with it. He seems to be dancing on the summit (his third eight-thousander).

Once more the line of the horizon widens out. The layers of mist have not evaporated, but have grown thin and transparent. Feeling I am being urged beyond the horizon, my dog-tired body grows light. I now feel that the summit on which I stand is more than mere earth beneath my feet.
(Reinhold Messner)

Descending from the summit in mist, snowdrift and storm, Reinhold Messner and Michl Dacher meet Friedl Mutschlechner, Alessandro Gogna and Robert Schauer on their way up.

My ability to make conscious decisions seems to have dissolved or to have become deeply-embedded within me. And my 'animal' instinct takes over and does what it has to. (Reinhold Messner)

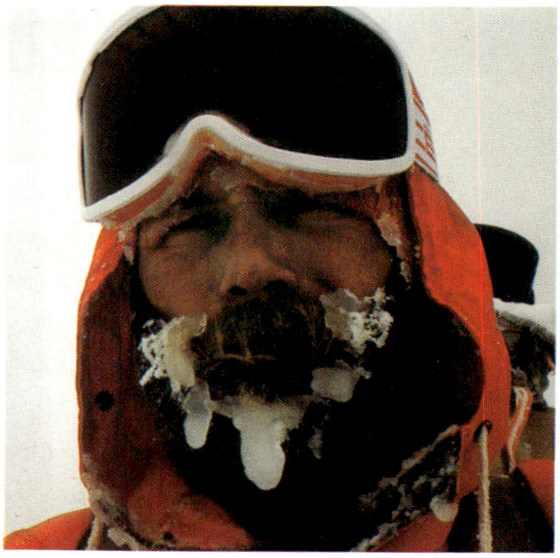

Robert Schauer, Friedl Mutschlechner and Alessandro Gogna (above, left to right) in repeated attempts on the summit, one time get as far as the last bivouac tent, which Messner and Dacher have left standing for those coming after. But there is no further successful summit ascent.

Experience told them that only cold, snow and bad weather could defeat them on the summit slopes. From the outset they reconciled their ideas to failure.
(Reinhold Messner)

After two months in the wilderness the expedition treks slowly back to civilisation. In the hot sulphur springs at Askole the team take their first bath.

When I look up at the summit, to that point where all the lines run together, it is as if all the loose ends inside me were also joined together.
(Reinhold Messner)

Left: Reinhold Messner and Michl Dacher after their summit climb. This expedition was the first time they had climbed together. It was not prearranged that these two would be the first and only summit team. Only during the course of the climb did chance throw them together.

Below: From the first, K2 has proved most accessible from the east. Left, in profile, the Abruzzi Ridge, named after the Duke of the Abruzzi who recognised it as the ideal ascent line at the beginning of the century (– – –). In the centre is the ridge by which an American expedition under the leadership of James Whittaker put four men on the summit in 1978 (—— —— showing first two camps).

The mountain filled the whole end of the valley, with nothing to draw the attention from it. Its lines were ideally proportioned and perfectly balanced, and its powerful architectural design was adequate to its majesty without being heavy. But the steepness of its sides, and its glaciers, were appalling. Its rocky wall was 12,000 feet in height. And as the Duke and his companions gazed at it, minutely inspected and examined it with their glasses, their minds were assailed with increasing doubts as to its accessibility. There did not appear to be a single point at which it could reasonably be attacked.
However, the Duke decided to make at least an attempt upon it by the southern ridge.
(Sir Francis Younghusband)

Without having planned or agreed it beforehand, each of us had his own place in the narrow tent. Weeks of proximity in such cramped and remote conditions leads to a mutual trust, to a friendly attachment that's not in any way cliquish. (Reinhold Messner)

Any line on a mountain of this size is a Magic Line. (Mohammed Tahir)

The scale was too vast, for one to receive at once an impression of the whole. The eye could only take in single portions and was not fully conscious of the dimensions of the landscape. There was no standard of comparison. The glaciers and valleys were so well adjusted in their proportions to the surrounding mountains that it was hard to realize the true size of any object. The Italians would repeatedly fail in estimating heights and distances. They were in a world built upon proportions so incomparably larger than those of the familiar Alps that the judgment of even the most expert among them was found wanting.
(Sir Francis Younghusband)

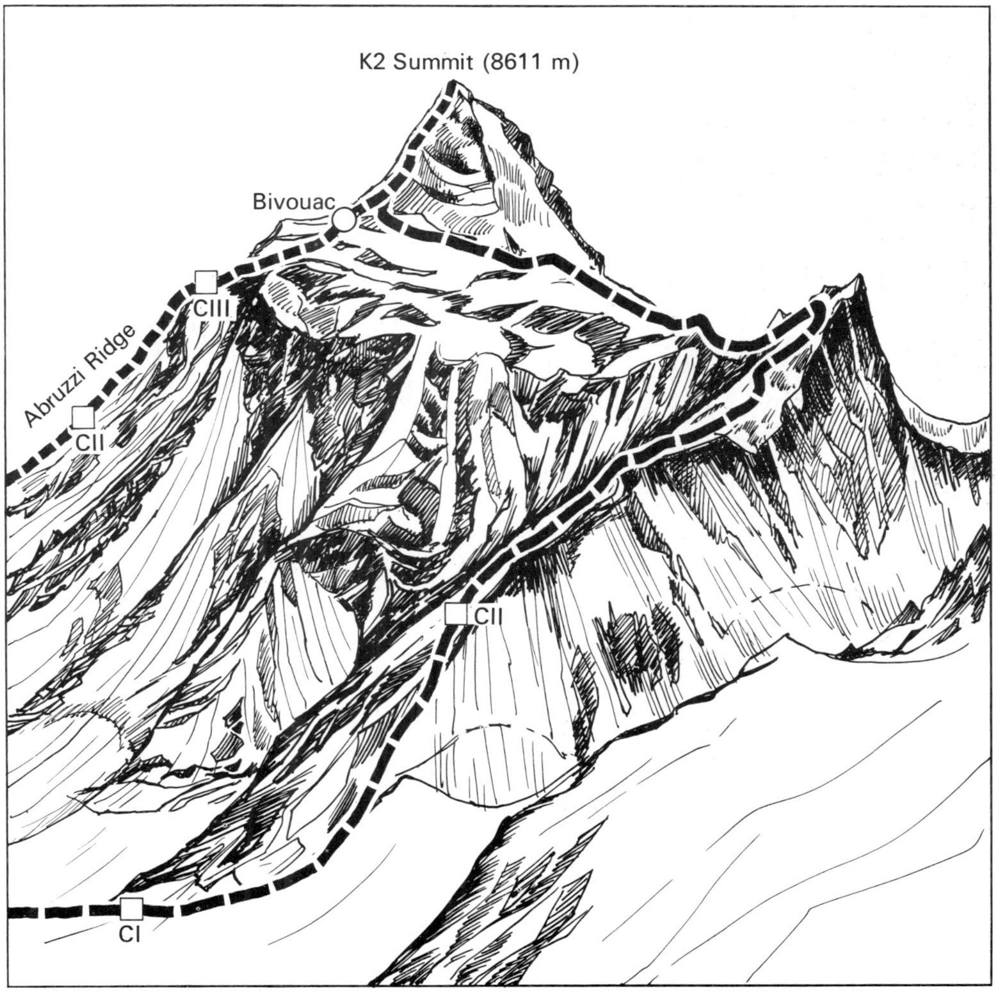

History of K2

Lift up your hearts, dear comrades! By your efforts you have won great glory for the Fatherland.
(Ardito Desio)

Ardito Desio, a sharp-featured drill-master, led his successful Italian K2 Expedition of 1954 like a brigade of black-shirts, behaving as if the conquest of 'Kappa Due' could erase all the debacles since the Battle of Custozza. He forced his team to endure forty days of almost incessant bad weather before a summit attempt was possible. And when one of 'my men', Mario Puchoz, died of pneumonia, he told the others, 'We can no more fittingly honour Mario's memory, than by ensuring triumph on K2, for which cause he has dedicated his life.' (Wilhelm Bittorf)

It may be wondered why so high a peak has no name. The reason is that, though high, it is not visible from any inhabited place.
(Sir Francis Younghusband)

Achille Compagnoni on the summit of K2.

1954 First Ascent

1953 was the year in which Everest was climbed for the first time by Edmund Hillary and Sherpa Tenzing Norgay. A year later two members of a huge, nationalistic Italian expedition – Lino Lacedelli and Achille Compagnoni – reached the top of K2, a success which prompted their leader to exclaim, 'Lift up your hearts, dear comrades! By your efforts has our dear Italy been presented with a splendid victory. You have demonstrated what Italians can achieve when they are inspired with a firm determination to succeed.'

From Hillary to the present day eighteen Everest expeditions have reached their goal; by the end of 1980 more than 110 people had stood on the highest point of the world, including four women (one each from Japan, Tibet, Poland and Germany). And the numbers grow with increasing impetus. One reason for this is that the 'Normal Route', apart from the Khumbu Icefall in its lower section, presents no great difficulties, technically, to the climber.

K2, on the other hand, has only been climbed three times since its first ascent: in 1977 by a large Japanese expedition who repeated the original route, the Abruzzi Ridge. They placed seven members on the summit – all wearing oxygen masks. In 1978 it was the turn of the Americans to reach the top, and in 1979, Reinhold Messner led a successful small expedition to K2. Yet, even this smallest, required a year of planning and a detailed knowledge of the mountain and its history. Before expedition members ever set foot on their chosen mountain, a talent for organisation is required, along with skills in negotiation and the ability to raise money.

1856 Montgomerie

In the year 1856, Captain T. G. Montgomerie, a triangulator with the Survey of India, saw 'a cluster of high peaks on the horizon.' He was looking at the Karakorum Range from a viewpoint 128 miles distant.

With the aid of his instruments, he measured the peaks and entered them in his log book, identifying them with a series of numbers, prefixed by the letter 'K'. The 'K' was merely an identification abbreviation used by the Survey to denote Karakorum. This mountain range in Northern Kashmir was important to London as it acted as a kind of buffer, protecting the plains of India from direct access from either China or Russia.

K1, K2, K3

Thirty-five summits in all were plotted by Montgomerie. Apart from 'K1', which was visible from a high mountain village and known to the Balti shepherds as Masherbrum (Snow Wall), the Survey of India had at first only discovered names for K3, 4 and 5, known collectively as Gasherbrum (Shining Wall). The other Karakorum peaks remained for the time nameless. As far as K2 was concerned, the Survey officials knew very little. No European had at that time seen it at close quarters, and Montgomerie was not even able to determine its height with certainty. However, this much was known: of the documented K summits, K2 stood the furthest north and, moreover, clearly overtopped all the others.

Godwin-Austen

Henry Haversham Godwin-Austen (British), the second European to visit the area, was the first to find his way into the heart of the Karakorum. Some years before him, the Munich born Himalayan traveller, Adolf Schlagintweit, had trudged beyond the high village of Askole.

Godwin-Austen, an officer with the Survey of India, accompanied by a few Baltis he had hired as porters, reached the tongue of the Baltoro Glacier, hoping to cross the so-called Mustagh Pass, that gap in the Karakorum crest that had already defeated Schlagintweit. The Englishman and his men were similarly beaten back, and returned to the Baltoro Glacier. They sweated a further fourteen miles up the glacier, which was strewn with gravel and lumps of ice. Europe's

We had just turned a corner which brought into view, on the left hand, a peak of appalling height, which could be none other than K2. Viewed from this direction, it appeared to rise in an almost perfect cone, but to an inconceivable height. We were quite close under it – perhaps not a dozen miles from its summit – and here on the northern side, where it is literally clothed in glacier, there must have been from fourteen to sixteen thousand feet of solid ice.
(Sir Francis Younghusband)

I kept quite silent as I looked over the pass, and waited to hear what the men had to say about it. They meanwhile were looking at me and, imagining that an Englishman never went back from an enterprise he had once started on, took it as a matter of course that, as I gave no order to go back, I meant to go on . . .
(Sir Francis Younghusband)

Col. Henry Haversham Godwin-Austen

longest glacier, the Aletsch, had by that time already been traversed along its whole length, but the Baltoro – into which a good many other glaciers also flow – seemed to stretch away into infinity. Godwin-Austen gave up. But before going back, he resolved first to climb a moraine hill which lay in front of the Masherbrum massif. Its scree slope offered a fine vantage point, and he became the first European to get a clear view of K2. Enquiring of his porters, he heard for the first time the local Balti name 'Chogori', literally Big Mountain. However, what Godwin-Austen saw was only the summit pyramid. Intervening ranges of mountains hid the foot and faces of the great giant.
In that same year, 1861, General Walker, Superintendent of the Survey of India, suggested that K2 be officially named Mount Godwin-Austen on the maps. The idea was not adopted, however, and the mountain continued to be known by its geometric-sounding keyname – K2 – largely because the Royal Geographical Society in London were unwilling to have to make a choice between Montgomerie and Godwin-Austen. For his part, Godwin-Austen was rewarded with the coveted Founders Medal of the R.G.S., bearing the inscription 'Karakorum Pioneer'.

1887 Younghusband, a Dragoon to K2

In the year 1887 a British lieutenant in the King's Dragoon Guards was confronted for the first time in his life with what was apparently an insuperable problem. With his Balti guide, a man named Wali; a Mongolian companion and others, Younghusband was making his way from Peking to India. Riding their camels mostly by night, they had reached Kashgar in Chinese Turkestan without difficulty. Then, instead of following the traditional caravan route to Leh in the Indian Ladak region, the Englishman resolved to be the first European to cross the Karakorum by its high mountain passes.
On the first of these, a 4750-metre pass, Younghusband's guide, Wali, confessed that he had forgotten the way ahead over the Mustagh Pass, the key part of the route to the south.
Younghusband went on ahead to reach the top of the next pass. Breasting the summit he saw something that made him 'literally gasp'. It was K2.
The men stumbled down the steep moraine into the glacier valley below, at the head of which apparently would be found the Mustagh Pass. (Mustagh is the Balti word for ice-mountains). At 5800 metres it was obviously much loftier than the other passes they had crossed. Towards midday Younghusband reached the climax of his journey from Peking. Standing on top of the pass, tired from his exertions in the thin air, what he saw robbed him of all desire to go on. Till then he had urgently kept pressing onwards, but now, below him on the south side of the Mustagh Pass, there was nothing but a dizzy 1000-metre drop, an ice slope beginning immediately under the col and as steep as the side of a church roof. Wali began to hack steps in the ice with his axe, doubtless to assuage any feelings of guilt at having brought his sahib to such a seemingly hopeless predicament. None of the men actually tied themselves to the rope that Wali was carrying. If one of them had slid off Wali's chain of steps, he would have whistled down alone without dragging the others with him. Younghusband tied his handkerchieves

William Martin Conway

Conway, surveying on Pioneer Peak.

Conway was knighted and later further honoured (as Lord Conway of Allington). His companion, Bruce, later General Bruce, commanded one of the legendary Gurkha regiments, and during the twenties led two of the earliest expeditions to Mount Everest. (Joachim Hoelzgen)

around his smooth-soled boots to give himself a better grip, and followed Wali down.

It was already growing dark when the party arrived on the Baltoro Glacier. Reaching Askole three days later, Younghusband continued from there to Skardu, where he was again able to get back into the saddle. He rode on to Srinagar, the capital of Kashmir to report to the British Political Agent of his Karakorum adventure. It has to be admitted that his countryman didn't appear all that interested in Younghusband's news however, 'Wouldn't you care for a wash?' he enquired.

The inhabitants of Askole had been excited to encounter their first white man, and had treated Younghusband with respect. But, his guide Wali, on the other hand, returning home after twenty-five years, went in fear of his life. The Baltis saw him as a traitor who had betrayed the secret of the Mustagh Pass. They regarded it, with reason, as a barrier protecting them from raiders from Tibet and Yarkand. Now the people of Askole feared an invasion, which indeed is what happened four years later.

1892 Conway, Art Critic, first on K2

The first K2 expedition left the high oasis of Askole in August 1892 under the leadership of a remarkable pair of men. Overall leader was the London art professor, William Martin Conway, his deputy, Lt. Charles Bruce. Bruce brought with him four porters, Gurkha soldiers he had detailed for K2. Without realising it, he had instigated a practice which became the norm for future expeditions, except that later on Sherpas or Hunza porters replaced the Gurkhas.

There were three more Britons, including the expedition's artist A. D. McCormick, and two German-speaking climbers completed the group: Oscar Eckenstein, an Austrian who had emigrated to England, and Matthias Zurbriggen, an alpine guide born in Switzerland but resident in the Italian mountain village of Macugnaga.

Conway was amazed at the length of the approach march. Camps had to be pitched along the way, between which the Gurkhas commuted back and forth, ferrying supplies. At the head of the Baltoro Glacier the sahibs finally reached an ice plateau, the confluence of glaciers that reminded William Conway of the Place de la Concorde in Paris, and to which he promptly gave the name Concordia.

Conway was quick to realise that any attempt to assail one of the bigger mountain giants was doomed to failure, and resolved instead to try two less threatening looking summits. He had, however, to do without the experience of Eckenstein who quit the expedition because he didn't like Conway's outmoded climbing ideas. Eckenstein had refused to tie onto Zurbriggen's rope because he was a firm believer in guideless climbing. You could take a cow up the Matterhorn, he once joked, if you were allowed to tie its legs.

Even from their equipment, you could see the difference between Conway and Eckenstein. Conway adopted a shoulder-high alpenstock, reminiscent of a bishop's crook, whilst Eckenstein, on the other hand, a gifted engineer, had already developed two of the climber's most important aids: an ice-axe of shorter length (85 cms) and ten-pointed crampons. With these fastened to his boots he gained an enormous advantage on ice.

Nevertheless, Conway's stay in the Karakorum was a great success. He climbed a subsidiary summit of a mountain he had christened Golden Throne, and equalled the height record of the Schlagintweit brothers from Munich. On top of Pioneer Peak, as he called it, Conway took barometer observations, did some plane-tabling and measured the pulse readings of his companions. He instructed McCormick to draw a panorama.

His return to London was a sensation. He had not only filled in one of the white spaces on Great Britain's colonial map, but with his journey into the ice-wastes of the Karakorum, the art critic-professor had also changed Victorian attitudes. Expeditions to high mountains now became socially acceptable.

1902 Crowley, an Anarchist on K2

Ten years after Conway's exploratory venture, a second expedition got under way to K2. Its participants had first of all to proceed alone, as the expedition's leader was stopped at the border of Kashmir. He was Oscar Eckenstein, and the authorities forbade him to go any further. It was said that the reason behind this was that William Martin Conway – who had in that same year been elected President of the British Alpine Club and who wielded considerable influence – did all in his power to put obstacles in Eckenstein's way. That, at any rate, was the opinion of the art-collector Guy Knowles, another member of the expedition.

Eventually, three weeks after his arrest, Eckenstein was allowed to follow after his advance party. This was indeed the first really serious attempt to climb K2, and Eckenstein's team was made up of some of the top alpinists of his day. There was the Viennese High Court Judge, Heinrich Pfannl, who had made the first ascent of the Hochtor North Face and a new route on the Dent du Geant in the Montblanc massif. His countryman, Dr Victor Wesseley, who had accompanied him on numerous climbs, was another member of the team. Then there was the Swiss doctor, Jules Jacot-Guillarmod, and the Irishman, Aleister Crowley, who described himself as 'journalist'.

Crowley was a friend of the otherwise fairly solitary Eckenstein. Both had done some difficult climbs in the Alps and in Mexico. Crowley, like Eckenstein, was condemned by the Alpine Club as being notoriously dishonourable. Eckenstein's pragmatism and Crowley's bizzare penchant for occult practices (he also smoked hashish) produced strange reactions.

Crowley arrived in Kashmir well ahead of the other participants. Following Eckenstein's advice he had come to learn something of Muslim customs. He wanted to master the laws of the Koran, and in particular those relating to hospitality, which could be useful on the expedition.

After his release, Eckenstein met up with the rest of the K2 group in Srinagar, the metropolis of Kashmir. In the meantime, Crowley had begun to recruit porters, including some men intended to climb to high level with the sahibs. Yet all attempts to teach the local Baltis, Brohpas or Pathans to climb came to nothing.

Aleister Crowley was very pleased with the Baltis he had hired for the march-in. He considered them to be loyal and honourable, though he reached quickly for the whip if he caught any of them pilfering salt or sugar, or items of equipment. On the other hand he was

Oscar Eckenstein, designer of crampons and ice axes.

Aleister Crowley, anarchist.

Crowley learnt Hindustani and the Balti dialect, and he let his beard grow. He was also very impressed by the Muslim custom of never touching the face with the left hand (to avoid ill-fortune), and from that time on he would only use his right hand.
(Joachim Hoelzgen)

There should be no difficulty in walking up the snow slopes on the east-south-east to the snowy Shoulder. From this point, which is just over 25,000 feet, the summit could be reached without question, given one fine day. (Aleister Crowley)

The Hunza represents a possible exception, this tough valley-dweller from the western part of the Karakorum. A few of them, as later expeditions to K2 and Nanga Parbat showed, proved to be extremely tolerant to altitude and also able to follow European and American mountaineers. Nevertheless most expeditions to K2 favoured employing Sherpas from East Nepal as high-level porters on the mountain. But in 1947, the year Pakistan became a separate state, entry permits were refused to Sherpas. As Buddhists, these bronze-featured men of Everest were undesirable, and were moreover considered to be pro-Indian. (Joachim Hoelzgen)

There remains the human problem, which cannot be got around with ultra-light titanium pegs, nor walkie-talkie radios, nor yet freeze-dried soups. In the traditional 'climber-collectives', this aspect would have been kept under strict control by military severity. Whereas in the loose, democratic teams of today, the moods, weaknesses and even the virtues of the participants succeed in bringing about self-realization. (Wilhelm Bittorf)

merely amused by those Balti farmers who joined the porter queues to collect rupees at the end of a march, even though they had carried no loads. These tricksters would come in from quite remote villages in the hopes of hoodwinking the sahibs – a game Crowley, with his oriental experience, quickly saw through. He knew how to handle porters.

Arriving at the high village of Askole, Victor Wesseley and Heinrich Pfannl were firmly of the opinion they could climb K2 in a mere three days. Like most newcomers to the Himalaya, they completely underestimated the enormous scale of the Central Karakorum. It took ten days for Eckenstein and his men to reach the end of the Baltoro Glacier. And then, standing on the Godwin-Austen Glacier, it was Crowley who misjudged distances. But what in fact he did do, was to instinctively recognise the technically most favourable route, the way by which K2 was eventually climbed in 1954. He spotted the potential of the 2000-metre Abruzzi Ridge, sloping at a mean angle of forty-five degrees up to the Shoulder.

When it came to climbing it, however, Crowley was outvoted by the others. Much to his disgust, they decided to attempt the North-East Ridge.

By the time they had reached a height of 6000 metres it was clear that the Balti porters would be unable to follow them over the steep ice, and the first attempt to climb K2 was aborted. Crowley, now more than ever disappointed, got into a quarrel with the gentleman-climber, Guy Knowles, and threatened him with a large-calibre revolver he carried in his rucksack. It came to a struggle on the brink of a precipice, before Knowles succeeded in wresting the gun from the violent Irishman.

One thing this bloodless episode did demonstrate, as if it were a foretaste of almost all following K2 expeditions, was how the isolation and cold of the mountain giants can shorten tempers and divide teams, who had arrived united in their resolution to tackle K2 together, or not at all.

The Swiss member, Dr Jacot-Guillarmod, considered Crowley neurotic, and for his part Crowley accused the doctor of being incompetent. Wesseley was universally disliked because of his habit of always gobbling up the best of the food, 'He would bend over his plate,' Crowley noted in his diary, 'and using his knife and fork like the blades of a paddlewheel, would churn food into his mouth with a rapid rotary motion.'

Crowley himself had incurred the wrath of the whole team early on, by persisting in bringing a great chest of books all the way. He threatened to quit the expedition if he were not allowed his reading matter.

Remarkably enough, this strangely assorted troupe were not yet finished. The two Austrians wanted to attempt the peak to the north of K2 at least, a peak they called Staircase (7544 m) now known as Skyang Kangri. Their ex-countryman, Eckenstein, however, favoured a continued siege on K2. As a compromise they attempted the saddle between the two peaks.

Then Pfannl fell ill. He was 'suffering from oedema of both lungs', diagnosed Crowley a non-medic, and indeed he was right, as it later proved. The climbers now gave up the attempt on the ridge between K2 and Staircase and hastily carried the gravely ill Pfannl down to the end of the Baltoro Glacier, where his condition immediately improved. The K2 historian, Galen Rowell, has written, 'Modern mountain doctors have pondered over why Pfannl's ailment was diagnosed as oedema instead of pneumonia.' Crowley, though a lay-man, had previously shown that he had an understanding of high altitude acclimatisation. 'You cannot live permanently in conditions unsuited to your organism,' he wrote. 'The only thing to do is to lay in a stock of energy, get rid of all your fat at the exact moment when you have a chance to climb the mountain, and to jump back out of its reach . . . before it can take its revenge.'

Sick and demoralised, Eckenstein's K2 crew retreated back to Askole, only to find cholera had just broken out there. Crowley himself was ill following a

To Günther Oskar Dyhrenfurth, the Himalayan professor, Aleister Crowley was a non-person. In (one edition of) his standard work 'Der dritte Pol', he even failed to mention that Crowley was ever a member of a K2 Expedition. 'Do what thou wilt shall be the whole of the law,' wrote the anarchic alpinist at one time. (Joachim Hoelzgen)

As a climber, Prince Luigi Amedeo of Savoy had the reputation of a pioneer. With the best climber of his day, the Briton Albert F. Mummery, he had climbed the Zmutt Ridge on the Matterhorn. His plan to scale Nanga Parbat in 1897 he abandoned when an outbreak of bubonic plague raged in Northern India. Instead he sailed to Alaska where with nine companions, he made the first ascent of Mt St Elias (5495 m). (Joachim Hoelzgen)

Sella, with a monstrous plate camera, understood how to combine the sharpened vision of the alpinist with the sweeping, stylised lines in vogue with the young artists of his day. He was also the first to feel the fascination of the South Spur of K2, long before Reinhold Messner saw the awesomely steep ridge as his 'Magic Line'. (Joachim Hoelzgen)

malarial attack, and Knowles and Jacot-Guillarmod went down with 'flu. Of the sixty-eight days they had spent on the Baltoro Glacier and K2, there were altogether only eight fine days. 'The average weather,' Crowley noted, 'was quite exceptionally abominable.' Dissension within the ranks split the team prematurely. Wesseley and Pfannl went on alone from Askole, while the four others, after having safely negotiated the narrow Braldo Gorge, settled for a more adventurous mode of travel. They built a raft of goatskins and floated from the village of Dassu down to Skardu.

Three years later Aleister Crowley made an attempt on 8597-metre Kangchenjunga, during which two porters and the Swiss climber, Alexis Pache, were killed by an avalanche.

Later Crowley wrote his memoirs, a 1058-page volume in which he defined his adventures as a means of self-discovery (two generations before Reinhold Messner propounded the same theory). Crowley's full-bodied portrayal of drug taking, ritual black magic and his frank attitude towards sex, outraged the puritan London press. The man – henceforward known as The Great Beast 666 – was accused of 'obscene attacks on the king, pagan orgies, blasphemy, obscenity, indecency, stealing, cannibalism, kidnapping, blackmail, murder and unspeakable crimes.' Even in the year of his death, 1947, Crowley was still denounced as 'the wickedest man in the world'.

1909 A Duke discovers the Key-Passage

On Good Friday 1909, eleven Europeans scrambled onto the quay in Bombay along with 262 numbered chests containing 13,280 lbs of luggage. This was the first of the mammoth Himalayan expeditions and had been planned in advance to the minutest detail. That was the only way that the aspired goal could be achieved declared the leader. He was Amedeo di Savoia, Duke of the Abruzzi, a nephew of King Victor Emmanuel II, and he sailed for India with ten other Italians, bound for the now legendary K2. His ambition

Luigi Amedeo of Savoy, Duke of the Abruzzi.

Vittorio Sella, pioneer of mountaineering photography.

One could not hope to complete so long and formidable a climb when from the very start one is faced with such overwhelming difficulties . . . K2 will surely never be climbed.
(Luigi Amedeo of Savoy)

Then, once again, it was a big Italian expedition which started the ball rolling in the Baltoro. In charge was Aimone di Savoia-Aosta, Duke of Spoleto, a nephew of Abruzzi's. The original intention was to make an attempt on K2 the chief aim, but on careful consideration the committee dropped this plan and laid the real emphasis on the scientific side, concentrating on a more exact study of the whole Baltoro tract, a new photogrammetric survey and the exploration of the Shaksgam. The credit for the varied and important scientific observations must go largely to Professor Ardito Desio, the expedition's geographer and geologist.
(Günther Oskar Dyhrenfurth)

was to get higher on one of the Karakorum giants than any of the assorted groups who had gone before. For this, he was the most likely man, with the most likely team for a possible success at that time. Already, in 1899, he had attempted to reach the North Pole and his expedition had come within two hundred miles of its objective before being turned back in a freezing blizzard. That adventure had cost Amedeo di Savoia the loss of some of his fingers through frostbite. Thin, with a penetrating gaze, the hardy Duke seemed incomprehensible to his fellow noblemen. His motives for such adventures were highly suspect.

This was the strongest team to have come to K2 so far. It included, for instance, the brothers Alexis and Henri Brocherel, two guides from Courmayeur who held the altitude record (set in 1907 when with Tom George Longstaff they reached 7120 m on Trisul). Another guide, Josef Pétigax, was also in the party; with him the duke had made first ascents of the Aiguille Sans Nom and the Pointe Margherita on the Grandes Jorasses, two of the finest tours of the day in the Mont Blanc massif.

Scientists had proved their worth on the duke's expeditions to Alaska and the Ruwenzori, so included too, were the geographer Filippo di Filippi, and his colleague Frederico Negrotto, a naval lieutenant. They would take charge of the route finding over the glacier fields. The team was completed by Vittorio Sella, a pioneer photographer, whose influence on mountain photography is still felt today.

The duke's party reached the start of the Baltoro Glacier on 19 May 1909. The number of porters had at times been as many as 500. Their loads had included 225 kilograms of rupee coins, since notes were considered unacceptable.

On this occasion the duke had left behind the field bedstead, he had tried out in Alaska. He had found then that the cold of the glacier accumulated under the mattress and chilled him more than if he had slept on the ground. In its place, the blue-blooded adventurer brought along a revolutionary invention – a sleeping bag, constructed of several layers: camel-hair, eiderdown, as well as goatskin, and all covered in a waterproof shell.

Eckenstein had experienced supply problems inasmuch as the porters could scarcely carry more than their own food requirements. To get around this the Italians bought sheep, mountain goats and chickens in Askole, and put them to graze on a patch of grass on the glacier. They were then slaughtered as required, and fresh meat was sent up to the higher camps.

At the end of May, seven years after Eckenstein was there, Europeans again reached the foot of K2. The duke immediately inspected the North-East Ridge, but it seemed to him to be too long and exposed, and the group now marched around the granite colossus to reach one of the glaciers on K2's western side. This the duke named Savoia Glacier, after his family's estate. The head of the valley led onto the North-West Ridge, a ridge which appeared to the duke to be not too steep. However, the ice slope leading up to the lowest point of the saddle, did appear insurmountable – blank ice shimmered through a thin snow covering. The duke named the saddle the Savoia Pass.

Disappointed, the Italians then turned their attentions to the south side of K2, which they had already seen from the Baltoro Glacier. A Base Camp was erected at 5000 m on the South-East Ridge. Amedeo di Savoia had discovered the way onto K2 by which, forty-five years later, men would first reach the summit – Italians like himself. This was the Abruzzi Ridge, as he not unnaturally called it.

With the Brocherel brothers, the duke toiled upwards for some 1000 metres. He was making for a prominent rock of yellowish-red colour, high above the Godwin-Austen Glacier, but they did-not quite reach it. They were one and a half vertical miles from the icy summit of K2 when they finally gave in. Filippi recorded that they had been obliged to yield to the conviction that K2 was inaccessible, not to be climbed.

Soon afterwards a small expedition ventured into the realms of the giants. With five companions, six Sherpas and only seventy-five Balti porters, the young American doctor, Charles Houston, moved up the Baltoro Glacier to attempt K2. It was the same year, 1938, when German mountaineers, with the support of the Hitler regime, were attacking Nanga Parbat at great expense, and even using a three-motor JU-52 aeroplane to ferry loads and airdrop supplies. (Wilhelm Bittorf)

Such an expedition is much more interesting – bigger ones are too hard on the nerves. (Charles Houston)

Dr Charles S. Houston

1938 Houston – a Cowboy on the Summit Pyramid

If K2 was indeed impregnable, as the duke predicted, the cream of expedition climbers after the first world war decided, therefore, to turn their attentions elsewhere. Further to the south-east – where Everest and Kangchenjunga seemed to offer more likelihood of success.

General Bruce, who had been with Conway to K2 in 1892, had already made a serious attempt on Everest back in 1922, during which expedition three men passed the 8000-metre barrier for the first time. The enterprise, however, ended in tragedy when a gigantic avalanche killed seven Sherpa porters.

By 1938 British climbers had launched half a dozen expeditions to Everest, and German mountaineers had twice been turned back on Kangchenjunga (which translated from the Sanskrit means the five holy treasuries of the great snows).

It was thus almost thirty years after the Italians, before the next potential K2 climbers arrived on the scene. They were American and led by Charles S. Houston, a medical student from New York. Houston had taken part in the first ascent of Nanda Devi in 1936. At 7860 metres Nanda Devi is the highest mountain in India. Houston had also himself led an expedition to Mt Foraker (5182 m) in Alaska.

His plan to attack K2 with the minimum possible outlay was in those days of 1938 something of a new conception in the Himalaya. On Nanga Parbat, for instance, German climbers had launched a veritable equipment-offensive. But Houston disdained this approach, considering that the extravagant use of men and material reduced mountaineering to a mere feat of engineering. He preferred to work with a small group, and this had the added advantage of being at the same time cheaper and simpler to organise. Houston's K2 expedition cost exactly 9434.03 dollars.

Five tried mountaineers and six Sherpas set off from Askole with seventy-five Balti porters for the trek to K2. They were: Richard L. Burdsall, who had climbed 7587 m Minya Konka in Tibet; the Alaskan veteran, Robert (Bob) Bates, and William P. House, who had made the first ascent of Mt Waddington, a remote massif which had previously defeated sixteen Canadian attempts. The team was completed by the Karakorum expert, Norman R. Streatfeild and a mountain guide-cum-cowboy from the Rocky Mountain state of Wyoming, Paul K. Petzoldt. Petzoldt had never taken part in an expedition before, but was the very epitome of fitness and condition. He had been the first climber to make a double traverse of the Matterhorn in a single day. On K2, this newcomer was going to prove to be the first man to reach the summit bulwark.

Houston's chances were good because for the first time in K2 history, he was employing six Sherpas. They included Pasang Kikuli, a survivor of the German Nanga Parbat tragedy of 1934.

The first problem was a strike of the Balti porters who were demanding more wages. (This was a weapon hitherto unknown to the Sherpas.) Houston solved the difficulty American-style, threatening to immediately discharge the strike leaders. Grumbling, the porters continued on their way with their heavy loads. In 1975 another American, James Whittaker, unleashed a diplomatic incident when he wanted to intimidate striking Baltis by setting fire to banknotes.

On 12 June Houston's little team reached K2. They skirted the Angelus, a fore-peak of K2, to reach the Savoia Glacier. Houston wanted to climb up to the Savoia Pass from the glacier, and from there look for a weak spot in the defences onto the North-West Ridge. Three times, however, they failed to reach the crest of the pass (6350 m). The climb over rock-hard ice proved too steep for the Sherpas.

While they were on the Savoia Glacier a tower of ice collapsed, burying a quantity of fuel supplies. Streatfeild, who had been to Hidden Peak two years before, took two Sherpas off on a march across Concordia and the Abruzzi Glacier to locate some fuel

Houston changed tactics when he noticed that too many men were on the ridge at the same time. Burdsall and Streatfeild went down off the mountain, along with three Sherpas. Only four Americans and three Sherpas remained on the ridge. That was an important decision.
(Reinhold Messner)

When House reached the top of the tower, he saw that the way on to the Shoulder was 'free from serious obstacles'. After having fixed ropes in House's Chimney, as it was known from then on, the bastion of K2 seemed pregnable for the first time.
(Joachim Hoelzgen)

The style in which the Americans made the difficult Abruzzi-Rib feasible, establishing their six camps, deserves full recognition.
(Günther Oskar Dyhrenfurth)

I felt that all my previous life had reached a climax. I believe in those minutes at 26,000 feet on K2, I reached depths of feeling which I can never reach again. (Charles Houston)

With a degree of luck our successors will reach the summit.
(Charles Houston)

left there by that expedition – fruitlessly, as it turned out. The dump was empty. Obviously porters from Askole who had been on the Hidden Peak venture, had come up again in the meantime to retrieve the fuel.

Houston's team refused to be deterred by this first rebuff. They now moved round to the base of the Abruzzi Spur. This was still the steepest ridge ever attacked in the Himalaya. For 2000 metres it rises skyward at an average angle of forty-five degrees. At a height of 7345 m. the spur ends at the so-called Shoulder, from where another ridge rises, crescentwise, for a further 600 metres to the summit pyramid.

Houston was well aware that the lack of oxygen in the air would take a lot out of his men. Even in Base Camp, the oxygen content of the atmosphere is only half that of New York; approaching the summit it would be barely a third.

High camps had to be erected in order to ensure a flow of supplies to the climbing group up front. Tents, for which platforms needed to be hacked out of the snow and ice on the steep ridge, were exposed to falling stones loosened by climbers active above them. Camp III at 6300 m had to be evacuated when people were climbing above it since it was showered with salvos of stones, like gunfire.

By 12 July, Camp III was stocked up with enough food for twenty days and Petzoldt had gone on to lead a steep section towards the proposed site for Camp V at 6550 m. Immediately above loomed the most difficult climbing proposition on the whole ridge, a vertical, fifty-metre high band of light limestone.

Since it was not possible to go around it, it could easily have spelt the end to the expedition, had William House not spotted a crack in the rock. It was just wide enough for him to wedge himself in with his hands and feet. He wormed his way upwards inch by inch, even though the crack was lined with a smooth coating of ice.

Petzoldt and Houston followed up and together erected Camp VII (7100 m). They were now only a skyscraper's height away from the top of the Shoulder. The Americans were blessed with better weather than any expedition before. For two weeks they had not been troubled by a single storm. But now, over the Nanga Parbat massif further to the south, dark clouds were massing. What should be done?

There were sufficient provisions in Camp VI for ten days, Houston reckoned. Should they go on up, he asked himself, bearing in mind the danger of becoming cut off if there was a snowstorm, since the descent down House's Chimney would then probably be too dangerous?

The four men gathered in Camp VI arrived at a compromise. Two climbers would go on from Camp VII, thrusting ahead as far as possible. The other two meanwhile, would transport the remaining stores to Camp VII and then retreat back to Camp VI.

On the morning of 20 July 1938, the four Americans and Pasang Kikuli humped loads up to Camp VII, which involved crossing a treacherously ice-covered slope. Houston and Petzoldt, who were the best acclimatised, remained in the top tent while the other load-carriers went back down as planned.

Then Houston and Petzoldt discovered that they had not brought any matches with them. How on earth would they be able to melt enough snow to quench the enormous thirst for fluids suffered at altitude? How could they cook, or thaw out the stone-hard Balti loaves?

In his pocket, Houston found he still had one box with nine matches in it. Yet it took three to light the stove. The men ate, melted snow, and drank tea. They wrapped up the warm pot of water and pushed it, like a hot water-bottle, to the foot of the double sleeping bag.

Another three of the remaining six matches were used the next morning. Outside it was cold, but there was no wind blowing. Houston and Petzoldt looked across to a cloud free Nanga Parbat. All the signs suggested the weather was remaining stable.

The crescent-shaped couloir ahead of the climbers was not very steep, but

Organiser and leader of the second American K2 expedition was the first-class German-American climber, Fritz H. Wiessner.
(Günther Oskar Dyhrenfurth)

They are all such a nice lot, taking everything from the easy side and hitting hard when necessary.
(Fritz Wiessner)

The German-American Fritz H. Wiessner.

was filled with soft powder snow that reached up to hip-height and drastically reduced their tempo. Finally at one o'clock, mounds of avalanche debris told them they had reached the base of the summit pyramid. It blotted out their whole view of the sky. Petzoldt, who had gone ahead to reconnoitre the start of the pyramid, now returned. They both decided to climb back down to Camp VII, where they had left their sleeping bags. Stars were already visible, even though the sun was still shining, when the two wet and chilled men reached their tent and began brewing tea. Trying to light the stove, their first match went out and the second snapped. They didn't get a light until the third. Barely half a mile short of their goal, the man from Wyoming and the other from New York, decided to abandon their attempt, because the next morning there would be no way either of them could prepare breakfast with all their matches gone.

1939 A Man from Saxony and the Great Gatsby – Disaster on K2

Dudley Wolfe, a dollar-millionaire who in 1928 had come second in a transatlantic yacht race, and who had just parted from his rich wife, seemed to embody F. Scott Fitzgerald's character, the Great Gatsby. This dazzling, well-built man, teamed up with a New American and together they planned a cool adventure. Fresh in the steps of the Houston Expedition, they wanted to go to K2, second highest mountain in the world.

Wolfe's partner in this venture was a man from Dresden who had emigrated to the U.S.A. in 1929, Fritz Wiessner was his name. He was a chemistry student who saw better prospects for himself in America, and also detected a whiff of the unhealthy times ahead in his native land.

With his departure Europe lost one of her best rock climbers. Wiessner had started climbing on the sandstone towers of the Elbe region. His ascent of the North Face of the Furchetta in the Dolomites with the Munich climber, Emil Solleder, had aroused attention in 1925. It was the first big Grade VI route in the Alps.

In America Wiessner created a sensation in 1937 when without any technical climbing aids, he succeeded in making the first ascent of that curious obelisk, the Devil's Tower, which rises out of the green parkscape of Wyoming. This 400-metre feature is the solidified core of an old volcano, whose rim has been worn away over the long passage of several million years.

Next to ocean racing, mountain climbing was Dudley Wolfe's declared passion. Wiessner knew that he had ascended various four-thousanders in the Alps, but he didn't, however, think the rich American capable of making it to the summit of K2. He was physically fit, certainly, but Wiessner warned him that his chances on the mountain were extremely slim. In the Alps, Wolfe had always climbed with guides and he lacked technical mountaineering know-how; also, he had never been on any expedition before. Wiessner, on the other hand, had been to Nanga Parbat in 1932, and had travelled widely, independently, over all manner of country. Wolfe was not to be dissuaded, however, and they began to put a team together. Wiessner had hoped to go to K2 the previous year with Houston, but had had to pull out for personal reasons. Now, he discovered it was not so easy to find another good team so soon afterwards. The strongest member of the 1938 expedition, Paul Petzoldt, was unable to return to India as there was a warrant for his arrest posted in all the police stations of the subcontinent. This was because on the return-march through India, Petzoldt had killed a man in the course of a quarrel.

Wolfe and Wiessner enlisted three students who had proved themselves in the Rocky Mountains: Chappel Cranmer and George Sheldon, both just twenty-one years old, and Jack Durrance, a medical student who had been working as a mountain guide during his holidays. Besides these, O. Eaton Cromwell was invited, a gentleman-climber who had been active in the Alps and in Canada.

Wolfe and the young people broke

They managed to set up a small high Camp IX among the lowest rocks of the summit pyramid, at 7940 m. On the nineteenth the pair made their attack on the summit. Wiessner later estimated the highest point reached as 8382 m.
(Günther Oskar Dyhrenfurth)

The American sahibs had not reckoned with the fact that for the two Buddhists, natural forces played a greater role than western ideas of moral worth. By Kitar and Tendup it was taken for granted that the Americans had perished in the blizzard or been buried by an avalanche. Instead of climbing up, they quitted Camp VI and climbed down.
(Joachim Hoelzgen)

In the lowest camp the four others in the expedition, who from the outset had been sickly and listless, had talked themselves into the steadfast conviction that Wiessner's long absence could only mean one thing. He and his two companions had died on the mountain. (Wilhelm Bittorf)

themselves in gently – for the first ten days they went skiing near Srinagar, where they also met up with their nine Nepalese Sherpas, led by Pasang Kikuli, who had already been to K2 with Houston's team.

On 31 May 1939, after the now-usual porter strikes, the group reached K2. Wiessner built up a textbook chain of camps along the Abruzzi Ridge. The original Camp III with its constant threat of stonefalls was bypassed. By the 6 July, Wiessner had set up his seventh high camp at the spot which had been Houston's highest campsite the year before.

Immediately, Wiessner climbed back down the long ridge to Camp II to make arrangements for the summit push, leaving only Dudley Wolfe up in Camp V. When Wiessner arrived at Camp II, however, he was confronted by a very disconsolate team. Sheldon had contracted frostbite in his toes whilst ferrying loads. Cranmer was afflicted with a serious heart disorder, and Cromwell categorically refused to move any loads up to 7000 metres. To cap it all, Durrance, on whom Wiessner had set his highest hopes, could not acclimatise to the altitude. Initially he had to commit himself solely to ferrying loads between Base Camp and the first two camps whilst he adjusted. The morale among all the men had sunk to a total low. Sheldon and Cromwell, the two most pessimistic about the whole venture, had already sent runners to Askole to order Balti porters for the return march. They planned to start pulling back down the Godwin-Austen and Baltoro Glaciers on 23 July. Wiessner had no wish to halt their plans. But meanwhile the five Americans (including Durrance) and seven Sherpas stocked up the high camps on the Abruzzi Ridge eventually gathering ten men together in Camp VI. A year earlier Houston had by this time only managed to get seven men high on the giant Abruzzi Rib.

On 13 July Wiessner, Wolfe and three Sherpas were in Camp VII with eleven loads. Pasang Kikuli, however, was not with them as he had decided to take charge of the other four Sherpas at the beginning of the South-East Ridge. The Sherpa Sirdar believed and feared that if he got frostbitten toes, his wife would no longer have anything to do with him.

A day later Camp VII was occupied, just below the crest of the Shoulder. Wolfe was in better form; the nearer he got to his cherished goal, the stronger he seemed to get.

Wiessner now sent two Sherpas back down to Camp VI where they were to fetch new loads for the summit attempt. Only Pasang Dawa, the strongest of the Nepalese, remained with the two sahibs.

Wiessner and Wolfe could not have guessed that a couple of thousand feet below, a fateful decision was being taken which was to trigger off the most bizarre chain of events in the history of the Himalaya.

It began with Durrance, who had already reached Camp VI where he again succumbed to altitude sickness. He decided to go back down to Camp II and commanded Pasang Kikuli and Sherpa Dawa Thondup to accompany him. The two other Sherpas, Tendrup and Kitar remained in Camp VI. During the next forty-eight hours it snowed continuously. Wiessner and Wolfe, at 7530 m high on the Shoulder ridge, were not advised that there were no longer any American climbers between them and Camp II. Sleeping bags, food and stoves were, however, lying in the three camps, ready for their eventual retreat.

After the two days of blizzard, Wolfe and Wiessner crawled out of the tent to make the first thrust up onto the summit pyramid. Powder snow lay waist-high in the great hollow basin. Nevertheless, with Pasang Dawa Lama following, they managed to establish Camp VIII on the snow at 7711 metres. Three days later, when again more new snow had fallen, the men stomped towards the summit pyramid over rapidly steepening ground to establish Camp IX on its slopes at 7940 metres, the highest bivouac on K2 to date. Dudley Wolfe, who was a big man weighing about 187 pounds sank into the snow almost to his chest and

The summit of K2, showing the highest point reached by Fritz Wiessner.

If only we had not lost our crampons – we could have walked right up this slope. (Fritz Wiessner)

Pasang Dawa Lama declared he was afraid of the wicked spirits who dwelt on the summits at night; really it was common-sense speaking. From the hardships endured by subsequent climbers on the other side of the rock barrier, Wiessner and the Sherpa could hardly have survived a summit attempt. (Wilhelm Bittorf)

We could not consider a bivouac. It was much too cold; only moving kept us reasonably warm. (Fritz Wiessner)

decided to turn back halfway and return alone to Camp VIII. He would wait there for better snow conditions. The fact that the two Sherpas, Kitar and Tendrup, didn't show up with the extra supplies didn't alarm Wolfe initially, although it had been agreed that they would fetch up loads from Camp VI.

Their leader, Pasang Kikuli, meanwhile, was fulfilling a fatal directive. Durrance had told him to clear the tents between Camps I and IV so that everything could be ready for a quick trek out to Askole. On 19 July, Durrance, Kikuli and Dawa Thondup arrived in Base Camp with thirteen sleeping bags. Durrance had left a note for Wiessner in Camp II congratulating him on reaching the summit, and advising that he had removed the sleeping bags so that the retreat could be got speedily under way.

Tendrup and Kitar, who Pasang Kikuli had sent back up to the sahibs, were the next to make a disastrous unilateral decision. They resolved to go only as far as Camp VII and from there to see if they could observe any signs of life above. If not, they would go down again, clearing the higher camps on the way, just as Pasang Kikuli had done lower down.

On the same day it was the 19 July 1939 Wiessner and Pasang Dawa Lama had a breakfast of hot tea in Camp IX. Wiessner felt strong enough to reach the summit before dark and with a day's food, he and Pasang set off. They reached the summit-bulwark at the top of the snow basin, from where it was some 575 metres to the summit dome.

Coming to a rock-band they found themselves faced with two possibilities. They could either go to the right, where the route led under a dangerous looking balcony of ice, poised ready to break off above their heads, or go to the left, where there seemed to be a gully in a precipitously steep wall of broken black rock. Wiessner, who always felt safer on rock, opted for the left hand choice, even though technically it appeared more difficult.

The day was surprisingly windless. Wiessner was even able to climb without his mittens, making full use of the sense of balance he had developed on the Elbe sandstone.

At 18.00 hours Wiessner reached what he later reported to be 8382 metres. Only another fifteen metres would have brought him access onto the summit ridge, which he didn't expect to present any serious climbing difficulties.

Then, suddenly, the rope went tight. Pasang Dawa Lama, who was belaying from below, would not pay out any more slack in the hemp rope. Wiessner called down that the worst difficulties were passed, but the Sherpa kept a tight hold on the rope, calling back, 'No sahib, tomorrow.'

Wiessner was quite dumbfounded. He wanted to go on to the summit and come down in the moonlight. But Pasang Dawa Lama feared that evil spirits would gather on the summit during the night. Wiessner, who knew this man to be a gifted climber and no weakling, was forced to give up.

Returning down the gully, the rope snagged on the crampons Pasang Dawa Lama was carrying on his rucksack whilst they were on the rock passages. Wiessner was about to sort out the muddle, when the two pairs of crampons were suddenly wrenched from the rucksack and vanished into the depths.

It was after midnight before Wiessner and his Sherpa got back to Camp IX. As tired as they were, a renewed summit attempt later that day seemed pointless, even though the morning dawned still and cloudless. Wiessner basked naked on his sleeping bag, acquiring an altitude sun tan.

Whilst this was happening, Sherpa Tendrup and two other Sherpas had come up above Camp VII. They shouted, believing that if the sahibs were still alive, they would suddenly emerge. Neither Dudley Wolfe, nor the two summiters a couple of hundred metres above him, heard anything. Tendrup took the answering silence as confirmation of his suspicions. Clearly the white men had been carried away by an avalanche. He began to

The catastrophe on K2 was as if it had been programmed.
(Reinhold Messner)

What had been going on here sabotage? (Fritz Wiessner)

At Camp VI, not a soul! No stove, no bags, no mattresses. We staggered on to Camps V and IV – the same terrific disappointment. With our last reserves, we continued to Camp II. Two Logan tents were up, but no living creature present . . . again no bags or mattresses. (Fritz Wiessner)

Both Wiessner and Pasang Lama were physically broken men. Their toes were frostbitten, and their limbs were little more than skin and bones.
(Galen Rowell)

One outstanding climber accompanied by one Sherpa right at the top of the mountain, and behind them a vast vacuum. From that moment an undertaking, itself of the most fearsome difficulty, was practically transformed into a forlorn hope.
(Günther Oskar Dyhrenfurth)

climb down with the others, clearing the camps and taking down the sleeping bags personally.

On 21 July Wiessner and Pasang Dawa Lama stood once more beneath the rock band on the summit pyramid. This time they had their sights set on the traverse around to the right beneath the overhanging ice. Without crampons, however, this was out of the question.

The two men turned back and rejoined Dudley Wolfe in Camp VIII. Wolfe appeared to Wiessner to have aged many years. 'Those bastards,' Wolfe cried, 'haven't come yet.'

He meant Tendrup's group who he had been expecting for days. For the last three, the American had only had meltwater to drink, which he collected during the day from the folds of his tent. Since no supplies had appeared, he was out of matches for lighting his stove.

The three decided to climb down to Camp VII without delay and stock themselves up. Wiessner left his sleeping bag behind in Dudley Wolfe's tent, believing there would be plenty more further down.

Then, during the descent, Wolfe stepped on the rope. The sudden jerk tore Wiessner from his stance and both men began sliding downhill, pulling Pasang Dawa Lama off behind them. At first Wiessner was unable to brake with the head of his ice-axe – the ice was too hard – and the climbers gathered speed as they approached the edge of the ridge. They were only forty metres from the edge when they finally slid to a stop in a sun-softened snowpatch.

The two tents at Camp VII stood open – their contents strewn across the snow. The sleeping bags Wiessner hoped to find there were gone.

Only now did they discover that Dudley Wolfe didn't have his sleeping bag either. The precious bundle had been torn from the top of his rucksack during the fall. The three men passed a dreadful night. Since they couldn't all fit into Pasang Dawa Lama's sleeping bag, they merely draped it around themselves. The next morning Wolfe, by now very feeble, preferred to remain in the sleeping bag where he was, while Pasang Dawa Lama and Fritz Wiessner hurried further down the mountain to Camp VI to find out just what had been going on.

They found, of course, that the whole ridge had been evacuated. 'Does one sacrifice human beings in such a way?' bewailed Wiessner in his diary. At Camp II he and Pasang Dawa Lama had to pass another night practically unprotected against the cold.

Hours later the two men staggered from the Abruzzi Spur onto the Godwin-Austen Glacier where they were met by O. Eaton Cromwell – who was, it transpired, out looking for their bodies.

Inwardly seething, Wiessner told the others that Dudley Wolfe wanted to take legal action against all those responsible for clearing the camps. Cranmer and Sheldon had by this time already left. Cromwell and Sherpa Tendrup, who had spread the killed-by-an-avalanche rumour, wanted to get away the next morning. Only the luckless Durrance and three Sherpas remained in Base Camp. They immediately tried to climb up to Camp VII to rescue Dudley Wolfe, but were unsuccessful. After that Kikuli came up with another plan. It required that he and Sherpa Tsering climb up to Camp VI in just one day. Up in that camp Sherpa Pintso and Pasang Kitar were already waiting, having gone up on the previous rescue bid.

On 28 July, Kikuli and Tsering did indeed manage to climb the 2300 metres in one day, an altitude gain the like of which had not at that time ever before been seen on an eight-thousander. The day after that, Kikuli, Kitar and Pintso finally reached Dudley Wolfe, who was by now a total wreck. He lay apathetically in his sleeping bag. He had not even left the tent to go to the toilet and excrement lay on the floor, tainting much of his food. Kikuli gave him a note from Wiessner, but Wolfe did not want to read it. He was too weak to go down just yet, he pleaded, 'Tomorrow,' he said, he would be prepared to go.

The three Sherpas climbed back down

For his new attempt on K2, Houston chose the seven strongest American climbers. But on the other hand, the climbing doctor had for the first time to manage on K2 without Sherpas: Pakistani officials sent the Nepalese away again at the border – they believed them to be pro-Indian and, moreover, Buddhist. Since then no Sherpas have worked as high-level porters in Pakistan.
(Reinhold Messner)

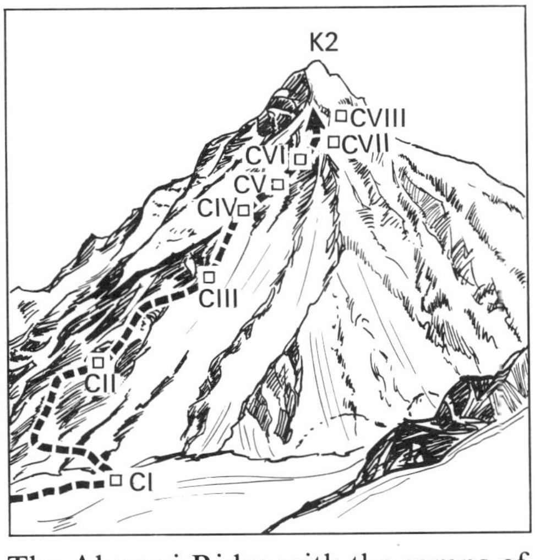

The Abruzzi Ridge with the camps of the 1953 American expedition.

to Camp VI where Tsering was waiting for them, and they told him of their conversation with Wolfe. The next day there was a snowstorm compelling them to keep to the tent, and when, the day after that, they set off again to see Wolfe, their intention was to escort him down, and if he still refused to come, to get from him a signed note to that effect.
Tsering, who had been completely knocked-up by the effort of the long climb up to the camp and who, therefore, preferred to stay behind in the tent, saw his companions disappear high on the Abruzzi Ridge. They didn't come back during the next couple of days, even though they had left their bivouac equipment in the tent with him. Shaking with cold and fear, Tsering now struggled back to Base Camp alone. Were Wolfe and his companions still alive?
'I am really in no shape to do it, and I may lose all my toes,' wrote Wiessner, yet, nevertheless, he set off again up K2 – this time alone. Pasang Dawa Lama was no longer able to accompany him.
However, Wiessner could only get as far as Camp II, before he had again to sit out two days of bad weather. After that, he turned back to Base Camp. On 9 August, he and Pasang Dawa Lama, all hope gone, left K2.
Dudley Wolfe and the tent in which he lay were not found by the expedition that came after – probably they had been carried away by avalanche. Of the three Sherpas, nothing was ever found except their sleeping bags in Camp VI. What happened to them remains a mystery.

1953 Multiple Accident on K2

Fourteen years after the Dudley Wolfe tragedy, Americans returned once more to K2. It was the first expedition to take place in a new political climate, since in 1947 the whole of the Karakorum had became part of the new Islamic Republic of Pakistan.
On 3 June, expedition members landed in the Indus Valley at Skardu. The political changes had drastically reduced the approach route. It was no longer possible to come from Srinagar in the Indian part of Kashmir as this would have meant crossing an armistice line, a result of the Kashmir War between India and Pakistan. For the alpinists, the alternative flight into the Indus valley clearly represented an enormous time saving. Only twenty-six days after having left the USA, the eight climbers had arrived at K2.
The route up the Abruzzi Ridge was familiar to the leader, none other than Charles S. Houston. He had in the meantime become a doctor and now had a practice in New York City. In 1950, twelve years after his first K2 adventure, Houston had brought off a second Himalayan pioneering feat, when he made the first reconnaissance of Mount Everest from the south. [Ironically, five days before landing in Skardu, Mount Everest was climbed for the first time – by the Khumbu Route explored by Houston and Shipton.]
When the eight climbers (who included the Briton, Tony Streather) polled a secret vote to see who should lead the summit attempt, they came up with George Bell and Bob Craig as the first pair, with Art Gilkey and Pete Schoening to follow them. None of these four younger expedition members had previous Himalayan experience. The veterans, on the other hand, came bottom of the vote. There was Charles Houston himself and Bob Bates (the 1938 tandem); then Tony Streather, who had made the first ascent of the Hindu Kush giant, Tirich Mir (7700 m), and he was to be partnered by Alaska-climber Dee Molenaar.
Houston's team quickly stormed the Abruzzi Ridge and believed themselves to be no more than forty-eight hours from the summit when Pakistan's most devastating monsoon brewed up. They experienced the worst winds and blizzards ever since climbers had begun attempting to climb K2. During the first day, Houston's men stayed tucked up in their sleeping bags and dressed in everything they had in Camp VII at 7700 m, where they were all gathered together. Driven snow forced its way through the closed doors of the tents;

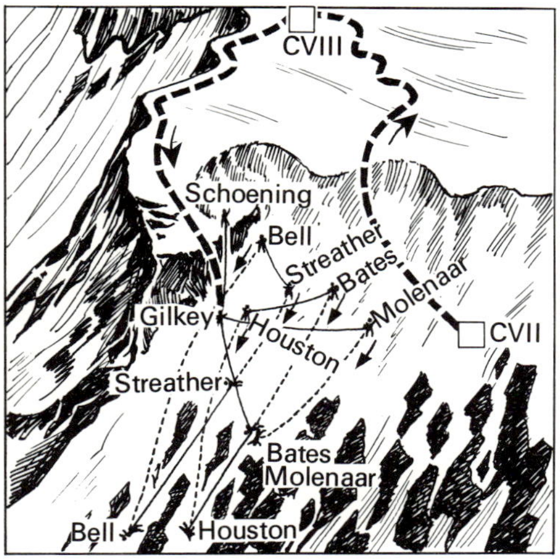

The mass fall in 1953.

These wearied men contemplated without dismay carrying a helpless body down cliffs which were hard and dangerous enough to tax a healthy, unladen party. . . None thought of leaving him and saving themselves – even though he would probably die of his illness. (Charles Houston)

Then it happened. George Bell, hands and feet numbed by the cold, slipped down the ice slope. His rope pulled taut on Tony Streather, who was whipped into the air like a fly. (Galen Rowell)

Pete Schoening

the hurricane made it impossible to keep any stoves alight. Houston knew that they would get very thirsty trapped in this snow-hell if they were not soon able to melt some of the white stuff.

To make the snow palatable and more nutritious they mixed it with powdered milk and jam. They hugged the cold mixture to their bodies to warm it and make it possible to swallow it at all.

What happened next was every Himalayan climber's nightmare: the storm ripped the tent belonging to Bell and Houston. In icy-stiff boots, they crawled over to join Bates and Streather. It was so cramped in the tiny tent that they could not all sit up properly inside.

Their trials had, however, only just begun. On the sixth day, Art Gilkey, a Professor of Geology from Colombia University, forced himself outside the tent and promptly collapsed.

'I've had this charley-horse in my calf for a couple of days now,' he said. 'It's sure to clear up in another day isn't it?' Houston took a look. What he saw he had till then only seen on elderly patients: Gilkey was suffering from thrombo-phlebitis. The veins in his calf were so inflamed that the danger of occlusion was acute. In New York, Gilkey would have had an immediate operation or been treated with anti-coagulants to prevent blood clots forming. On the Shoulder of the Abruzzi Ridge, however, Gilkey's chances were hopeless. Houston's team decided to move down at once, carrying Gilkey back to Base Camp.

Seven haggard and all but dehydrated alpinists carried Gilkey down through the swirling snow on a stretcher they constructed from the tent that had been destroyed in the storm. Beneath the heavy snow, the South-East Spur of K2 was coated in hard ice.

On 9 August, Gilkey developed an embolism in both lungs. He was coughing badly and his pulse had risen to 140 beats per minute. Since the wide slope below the Shoulder was in danger of avalanching, the men decided to heave Gilkey over a steep rock rib, which led fairly directly down to the narrow platform of rock on which Camp VII was situated.

Such was the scene when blond Pete Schoening found himself responsible for the most difficult stage of Gilkey's rescue. Gilkey had to be lowered over a fifteen-metre cliff which ended on a steep ice slope. In order to safeguard himself, Schoening constructed a special belay. He first of all rammed his axe well down in the ice above a humplike boulder of rock, a short way above the cliff-edge. Then he ran the rope from himself up around the shaft of the ice-axe. Should Gilkey start to fall, then the strain on the rope, Schoening reckoned, would merely press his own body closer to the boulder. In this manner he could not only halt Gilkey's fall, but the two fixed points – axe and rock – would with luck be prevented from bursting out of the ice in the manner of a champagne cork.

Cautiously Schoening, physically the strongest member of the expedition, lowered Gilkey down the rocky buttress. No problems. The other men could now follow, one after the other, and pick up Gilkey at the bottom, from where he could easily be transported to Camp VII which was only ninety metres away.

Then it happened. George Bell, whose hands and feet were frozen and numb, slipped.

The rope tautened with sudden speed, pulling with it Tony Streather, and then snagged a second rope, the one linking Charles Houston and Bob Bates. These two were immediately torn from the slope, also Dee Molenaar, having completed an abseil, was now connected to Art Gilkey, when suddenly he yelped as he, too, was whisked off his feet and joined the downward plunge.

The mass fall was headed directly towards the big drop, below the Shoulder, where the edge of the Abruzzi Ridge swept 2500 metres down to the Godwin-Austen Glacier. Bates and Houston tumbled first, followed by Bell, who shot through the whole group. Only Bob Craig – ski instructor and philosophy student – looked sure to survive. He was the only one un-

It is within the realms of possibility that Gilkey, appraising his hopeless condition and the risk that his companions were taking to save him, cut himself loose from the slope.
(Galen Rowell)

Prof. Dr Ardito Desio, leader of the successful Italian K2 Expedition of 1954.

In 1954 it was the chance for a large-scale Italian expedition. It was well known in Italy that if they did not succeed in 1954, the Americans would be having another turn in 1955. This was the critical hour, and they acted accordingly. The financing of this enormous expedition, which was also supported by government contribution, required about 120,000 lire (around 200,000 dollars).
(Günther Oskar Dyhrenfurth)

roped, and was already on the platform housing Camp VII. Horrified, he watched the tangle of men and ropes gaining acceleration. Suddenly in a white cloud of crystals, the fall was halted. The rope pulled tight, like the string of a saracen's bow. Schoening later declared it had, 'shrunk to half its diameter.' What had happened? The ropes of the two falling pairs had caught Schoening's rope, which as last man, was as taut as a snare. Even Molenaar and Bates, who had already reached the edge of the ice slope, were halted. Peter Schoening's hands were like stewed meat – the rope racing through them had even scorched the thick Indian gloves he was wearing.

What was the damage? George Bell, a Physics' Assistant at Cornell University, feared his fingers were frostbitten. Art Gilkey lay motionless at the start of the traverse to Camp VII. Worst of all, Charles Houston appeared to have suffered a head injury. He was lying in the snow, and it was Bob Bates who was the first to reach him. Bates ordered him to come with him, but Houston didn't respond.

'Where are we?' was all he could say. Bates made just the right move, 'Charlie,' he said sharply, 'if you ever want to see Dorcas and Penny again, then climb up here right now.'

The mention of his wife and daughter did the trick. The expedition's doctor/leader dragged himself to Camp VII with Bates.

Gilkey, meanwhile, was anchored to the steep slope by two ice-axes. His companions had first of all to enlarge the tent platform so that there would be room for the whole team. When Bates, Craig and Streather went back to the place where they had last seen Gilkey, it was empty. Gilkey had vanished. Along with both the axes to which he was secured.

Houston spent all that night in Camp VII in a delirium.

'I know all about these things,' he would tell the others, 'I have studied them. In three minutes we'll all be dead if you don't let me cut a hole in the tent.'

Continuing down the next day, the beaten men found scraps of rope and clothing, and some bloodstains. Otherwise there was no clue as to what had happened to Gilkey.

The Americans kept going for ten hours a day, which must have been terrible agony for Bell. His discoloured feet were so swollen he had to cut open his boots.

Above Camp II the Hunza porters raced to help them. They had already given the men up for dead; now they escorted them down to Base Camp. For the first time in twelve days they had warm food and tea, dry sleeping bags and their frozen feet and hands were massaged.

Where the Godwin-Austen Glacier meets the Savoia Glacier, the Americans built a memorial cairn for Gilkey and the dead of the Wiessner expedition. 'We came as strangers,' said Houston, 'we are leaving as brothers.'

1954 'Vittoria' – the Conquest of 'Kappa due'

Only one year went by before the Gilkey Memorial pyramid bore another inscription: Mario Puchoz 20.6.1954.

An Italian expedition brought honour to the Fatherland with the ascent of K2. The French had already climbed Annapurna, the British Everest and on Nanga Parbat, Hermann Buhl had hoisted his country's flag.

Leadership of this important expedition was entrusted to Professor Ardito Desio, the celebrated Milan geologist, Karakorum expert and administrator. The climbing team was extraordinarily strong: Erich Abram, Ugo Angelino, Walter Bonatti, Achille Compagnoni, Cirillo Floreanini, Pino Gallotti, Lino Lacedelli, Mario Puchoz, Ubaldo Rey, Gina Solda, Sergio Viotto, Dr Guido Pagani and the cameraman, Mario Fantin.

They experienced awful weather and as a consequence, had great difficulties with their porters. June, normally a good-weather month, this time confronted them with heavy snowstorms which hindered any work on the Abruzzi Rib.

The final success was due to the relentless determination of two magnificent climbers – Achille Compagnoni, from Val Furva, and Lino Lacedelli, of Cortina d'Ampezzo. Admittedly, they climbed 'on the shoulders' of their team-mates, as did the whole Italian undertaking on those of the 1938, 1939 and 1953 American expeditions.
(Günther Oskar Dyhrenfurth)

I had the feeling that a third person followed us: a woman who slowed down my pace when I was moving, and when I stopped, exhausted, prompted me to go on.
(Achille Compagnoni)

The triumphant K2 expedition was a well-organised example of a 'war of equipment', carried to its conclusion by every member of a great team.
(Günther Oskar Dyhrenfurth)

Achille Compagnoni and Lino Lacedelli, the first men to climb K2.

We were pinned in Camp VI for ten whole days, cut off from the world. Then at last we were able to come down. To go up would have been senseless because food supplies were very meagre, but above all fuel was precious. (Ludwig Greissl)

Mario Puchoz fell ill with high altitude cough and laryngitis; inflammation of the lungs followed. He died on 20 June in Camp II, the sixth victim of K2. But the struggle went on. In two months, the team experienced over forty stormy days. But gradually the high camps were pushed up. On 25 July, Camp VII was established on the Shoulder. On 28 July the advance party, comprising Compagnoni, Lacedelli, Abram, Gallotti and Rey, reached the site destined for Camp VIII, near the top of the Shoulder.

On 30 July Compagnoni and Lacedelli struggled to the foot of the dark girdle of rock and erected an assault tent at around 8050 m, ready for their final bid. The South Tyrolean, Abram, with Walter Bonatti and the Hunza porter, Mahdi, attempted to bring up oxygen apparatus and provisions, but were unable to reach Camp IX by nightfall. Abram immediately turned back and succeeded in returning to Camp VIII, but Bonatti and Mahdi were forced to spend the night out in the open at almost 8000 metres.

Desperately they sought Compagnoni and Lacedelli. Alarmed, Bonatti repeatedly shouted their names. Why did they not answer? Mahdi was in such a state, he was bellowing unintelligibly, like a madman.

Then, suddenly, a light glinted from below the rocks to the right. It was Lacedelli. 'Have you got the oxygen,' he called.

'Yes,' answered Bonatti.

'Good. Leave it there and go back. Go back!'

'But I can't,' hollered Bonatti, 'Mahdi won't make it. He's out of his senses!'

Whilst this was going on, Mahdi stood up and groped around in the darkness before lunging off towards the steep ice slope from where the torchlight was shining. Suddenly, the light disappeared. Bonatti thought his friends were coming to help him. But he waited in vain. Again and again he called, but nobody answered. Then the terrible reality of the situation slowly dawned upon him.

Sudden and violent gusts of wind covered Bonatti and Mahdi in icy powder snow, plastering their faces and getting in under their clothes. With difficulty they managed at least to protect their mouths and noses with their hands, so as not to suffocate. They clung to life like shipwrecked sailors to a log.

The next morning the wind eased. Despite a clear sky, Bonatti could not make out the tent of the summit pair. He dug the oxygen equipment out of the snow and left it standing there. Then he began to go down. Mahdi had already scuttled off at first light.

The same morning Lacedelli and Compagnoni climbed down a bit and discovered the oxygen in the snow. They made ready for their summit climb. They were unable to scale the gully which cut through the rock band since it was choked with deep snow. Compagnoni tried the rocks, but fell off and landed back in the snow. Lacedelli took off his gloves and scrambled up a thirty-metre cliff above the Bottleneck. The rock wall was covered in deep soft snow.

By the time they had put the great seracs far below them, the oxygen flasks were empty. Compagnoni and Lacedelli tore off their face masks; they didn't suffer any ill effects, no collapse. So, onwards! With tremendous determination, they toiled up over the endless snowfields until finally at 18.00 hours on 31 July, stood atop the summit.

After half an hour's rest, they set off on what was to prove an eventful descent, a series of potentially dangerous incidents, one after the other: a snow slab breaking away, one of them falling and pulling off the other; the loss of an ice-axe; frostbite; a huge crevasse to cross into which Compagnoni tumbled and fell fifteen metres. Lower down, Compagnoni slipped again, this time whistling down 200 metres to the brink of the great ice precipice at the eastern end of the Shoulder, where by extreme good fortune he came to rest in some soft snow.

1960, 1975, 1979 – Three Unsuccessful Expeditions

The German–American K2 Expedi-

K2 from the north-east, left the Abruzzi Ridge, to the right the American 1978 route.

The summit pyramid of K2, showing where the Poles turned back.

Ichiro Yoshizawa, leader of the Japanese monster-expedition of 1977.

tion of 1960 was led by Major W. D. Hackett. His companions included the German climbers Ludwig Greissl, Dr Wolfgang Deubzer, Günther Jahr, Herbert Wünsche and Americans, Davis Bohn and Lynn Pease. They were caught in a storm at the end of the Abruzzi Ridge and unable to progress any further.

James Whittaker's 1975 expedition to the North-West Ridge didn't even get as high as that. Nor was the summit reached by an extraordinarily strong Polish expedition attempting the North-West Spur in 1976, but nevertheless, that expedition led by Janusz Kurczab ranks among the most outstanding achievements on K2.

The nineteen Poles brought experience and determination to the ridge first attempted by Eckenstein. They had overcome the main difficulties in the central section and by 12 August were at a height of 7900 metres, below the summit pyramid, and had set up a last camp (VI). Two summit attempts followed: on 14 August, when Leszek Cichy and Jan Holnicki-Szulc had to give up below a rock band at around 8200 metres; and on 15 August, when it was the turn of Eugeniusz Chrobak and Wojciech Wrz, who managed to get a good 200 vertical metres higher. They were stopped not by the deep snow nor the Grade V rock-climbing, nor yet the avalanche danger, but rather because they were too late, their oxygen stocks were at an end, and the weather was uncertain. At 18.00 hours they abandoned their attempt.

1977 The Japanese

When the Japanese came, they launched a mass attack on the mountain. They brought no less than forty-two climbers, so that there would always be a number of fresh teams, ready to scurry up in relays, constantly relieving each other. Balti porters brought what material was needed for the onslaught up into Base Camp, and high-level porters from Hunza, Skardu and Kapalu carried it on as far as the last camp under the summit pyramid.

The three Japanese who were first to reach the summit (by the Abruzzi Ridge) duly and dutifully reported back, 'At 18.50 hours we stood at last on the summit. We could hear the cry of joy of our leader, his deputy as well as all the members back in Base Camp, over the radio. At last the efforts of the forty-two had been rewarded.'

1978 The Americans

The Americans, too, put four men onto the summit of K2 in 1978. They started out with more than a dozen climbers, including three women (two to climb and one as Base Camp cook). Here, too, most of the team were really mainly engaged in preparing the route for the two summit ropes, so that they would be as fresh as possible for the final phase.

The fourteen Americans climbed the

It was like a war of attrition. Never before in the mountains was there a battle of such proportions.
(Robert Paragot)

At the critical moment the French lacked the courage to press on into the unknown nothingness above them.
(Reinhold Messner)

'It's Hell up here!' (Ivan Ghirardini)

mountain by a line which was in its lower sections a new route (the Polish ridge), but when they reached the decisive upper third, they were forced to swing across to join the Italian route. Of the four men who forged their way to the summit, two climbed completely without oxygen.
A few months earlier Chris Bonington had been defeated on the opposite side of K2. With a tough team, many of whom had been on the successful ascent of the fierce South-West Face of Everest in 1975, he was attempting the West Ridge. The attempt was abandoned after the death of Estcourt under an avalanche.

1979 French on the South Pillar

Two months after Reinhold Messner's lightweight success on K2, a large French expedition with 1700 porters failed in their attempt on the mountain.

1980 Further British Attempts

Four British climbers – Pete Boardman, Dick Renshaw, Doug Scott and Joe Tasker – arrived in 1980 to have another try at the West Ridge route. With so small a team, they experienced difficulty in ferrying sufficient equipment and decided, having reached 7010 m, to abandon this line.
Boardman, Renshaw and Tasker then decided to attempt the Abruzzi Ridge route but were prevented by appalling weather conditions.

K2 – Chronicle

Geographical Location of K2: 35° 52′ 55″ N. Latitude, 76° 30′ 51″ E. Longitude

1272–1274 The Venetian, Marco Polo, passes close by the Karakorum on his journey to the Great Kublai Khan in China.
1835–1838 G. T. Vigne undertakes extensive journeys in Kashmir, Ladakh and Baltistan. His detailed descriptions also cover part of the Karakorum.
1856 The Munich-born explorer, Adolf Schlagintweit, becomes first European to penetrate the Baltoro region. In August 1856 he visits Askole and ascends the (Eastern) Mustagh Pass.
1856 Captain T. G. Montgomerie, an officer of the British Survey of India, spots a 'cluster of high peaks' in the inner Karakorum from a distance of 128 miles. He numbers the recognisably highest as K1, K2, K3 etc. (The K stands for Karakorum.) It is only much later that the local name Chogori becomes known, but fails to gain international usage. The giving of names to peaks to commemorate gentlemen of the Survey of India (such as Montgomerie or Godwin-Austen) is dropped.
1861 The British Lt. Henry Haversham Godwin-Austen, an officer with the Survey, explores with a handful of Baltis, a large section of the Western Karakorum and its glaciers. It is him we have to thank for the first map (1:500 000) of the area, as well as the first description of the approaches to K2.
1887 Lt. Francis Younghusband (later Sir) an Indian-born, British Officer and a very capable Asian explorer, makes one of his far-reaching journeys in the Karakorum and is overwhelmingly impressed by the huge scale of the mountains and glaciers. He crosses the (old) Mustagh Pass.
1892 William Martin Conway (later Lord Conway of Allington) makes an exploratory journey to the foot of K2.
1902 An expedition under the leadership of Oscar Eckenstein attempts to climb K2 by its North-East Ridge. The Upper Godwin-Austen Glacier is explored and Windy Gap reached. Probable highest height reached on K2 – 6200 metres.
1909 Luigi Amedeo di Savoia, Duke of the Abruzzi, on his expedition to K2 recognises in the South-East Spur (later the Abruzzi Spur/Rib/Ridge) the most favourable ascent route. The expedition doesn't get much above 6000 metres. Valuable photographic results.
1929 Prince Aimone di Savoia-Aosta, Duke of Spoleto, abandons his plan to climb K2 and concentrates on scientific work. A reconnaissance party climbs to the foot of the Sella Saddle in order to study the Abruzzi Ridge.
1937 The Shaksgam Expedition which included Eric Shipton and Michael Spender, maps and photographs the north side of K2.

K2 from the north.

1938 The American Charles Houston leads a small expedition to K2 which climbs the South-East Spur – the Abruzzi Ridge – to a point between the Shoulder and the Black Pyramid. This is the first time the key passage of the Abruzzi Ridge has been climbed. Although not achieving the summit, this first small expedition can be considered an important success.
1939 The German-American Fritz Wiessner comes within a few hundred metres of the summit of K2 in an assault with Pasang Dawa Lama. During the descent Dudley Wolfe dies. Attempting to rescue Wolfe, three Sherpas are lost without trace.
1953 Charles Houston leads his second expedition to K2. The weather turns bad

after a height of 7500 metres has been reached. The whole team retreat. Art Gilkey falls seriously ill. In an attempt to rope him down, the whole team is nearly lost in a multiple fall. It is a miracle they are halted by the ropes. Art Gilkey, however, disappears.

1954 A large-scale Italian expedition climbs K2 after a long build-up of camps on 31 July. Lino Lacedelli and Achille Compagnoni reach the summit via the Abruzzi Ridge.

1960 Major W. D. Hackett leads a K2 expedition which besides Americans also includes German climbers. They attempt the same route as the 1954 climbers, but don't get much further than the Black Pyramid.

1975 James Whittaker, the first American on Mount Everest, fails with a strong American team, in his bid to climb K2 from the Savoia Pass.

1976 A Polish Expedition, led by Janusz Kurczab scales the North-East Spur to a point just below the summit. Technical difficulties, avalanche danger and a new snow force the team to retreat.

1977 A giant expedition from Japan climbs K2 by the Abruzzi Ridge. Two ropes including a local Hunza porter reach the highest point.

1978 The Pakistani authorities for the first time grant two teams permission to attempt K2. A British team lead by Chris Bonington abandons its attempt on a new route over the West Ridge when Nick Estcourt is killed in an avalanche. On the other hand, the American James Whittaker, this time on the North-East Ridge, is successful in putting two ropes on the summit.

1979 For the first time a small expedition successfully manages to climb K2. Reinhold Messner, abandoning his original plan to climb the South Spur ('Magic Line') for safety reasons, with his team climbs the Abruzzi Ridge to the summit. At the same time a large French expedition attempts the South Spur. They fail between the Mushroom and the summit.

1980 A very small British expedition having first attempted the West Ridge, twice reached 7900 m on the Abruzzi Ridge route. The first time they were forced to withdraw after being hit by an avalanche, and the second were turned back by blizzard and high winds.

Successful Ascents (to December 1980)

	Date/Year	Climbers	Route	Expedition/Leader
1	31.7.1954	Lino Lacedelli Achille Compagnoni	Abruzzi Ridge 9 camps	Italian Expedition (Ardito Desio)
2	8.8.1977	Tsuneho Shigehiro Takeyoshi Takatsuka Shoji Nakamura	Abruzzi Ridge 6 camps	Japanese Expedition (Ichiro Yoshizawa, Isaho Shinkai)
3	9.8.1977	Mitsuoh Hirishima Masahide Onodera Hideo Yamamato Ashraf Aman (Hunza from Pakistan)		
4	7.9.1978	Louis Reichardt James Wickwire	North-East Ridge to 7700 m, then Abruzzi Ridge (One pair climbed without additional oxygen)	American Expedition (James Whittaker)
5	8.9.1978	Rick Ridgeway John Roskelly		
6	12.7.79	Reinhold Messner Michl Dacher	Abruzzi Ridge 3 camps 1 assault camp	International Expedition (Reinhold Messner)

There have been fourteen specific climbing expeditions to K2. In the twenty-five years since the first ascent, fifteen climbers have reached the summit.

The fact that over twenty-five years only four expeditions have met with success, is proof of the difficulty of K2. Taking its absolute altitude, steepness and exposure into account, it is without doubt the most difficult of all the eight-thousanders.

To date there have only been two routes climbed, and the second of these the North-East Ridge is not a completely autonomous route, since just under the summit pyramid it joins the 1954 Italian route.

K2's various ridges – the South Spur, the West Ridge, the North-West Ridge and the North Ridge – represent the most difficult climbing problems that exist anywhere. The faces between are in places easier, but more hazardous.

The Expeditions to K2 (1892–1980)

	Year	Leader/Participants	Expedition/Organisation	Route/Remarks
1	1892	**William Martin Conway** (GB); **Lt. Charles Bruce** (GB); A. D. McCormick (GB); Matthias Zurbriggen (Switz); 3 Nepalese Gurkhas	First British Karakorum Expedition Patrons: Royal Society and Royal Geographical Society	First expedition with mountaineering objectives; outcome: valuable topographical and mapping work.
2	1902	**Oscar Eckenstein** (GB); Aleister Crowley (Ireland); Jules Jacot-Guillarmod (Switz); George Knowles (GB); Heinrich Pfannl (Austria); Victor Wesseley (Austria)	International Expedition Financed: George Knowles	Attempt on North-East Ridge; Pfannl taken seriously ill (pulmonary oedema); the climbers consider K2 unscalable.
3	1909	**Luigi Amedeo di Savoia, Duke of the Abruzzi**; E. Botta; Alexis and Henri Brocherel; 4 porters from Courmayeur; Filippo de Filippi; Frederico Negrotto; Joseph Pétigax; Vittorio Sella	First Italian Expedition 330 porters	First attempt on South-East Ridge, attaining a height of 5560 m; 7500 m reached on Chogolisa (7654 m) which remained world altitude record for 13 years; exceptional photographic coverage by Vittorio Sella.
4	1929	**Prince Aimone di Savoia-Aosta**: team includes Ardito Desio	Large Italian Expedition	Planned climbing attempt abandoned; extensive and varied scientific fieldwork accomplished.
5	1938	**Charles S. Houston**; Richard L. Burdsall; Robert Bates; William P. House; Paul K. Petzoldt; Norman R. Streatfeild; Sherpas	First American (small) Expedition Patron: American Alpine Club	First determined attempt via Abruzzi Ridge on which 7 camps were established.
6	1939	**Fritz Wiessner**; Chappel Cranmer; Eaton Cromwell; Jack Durrance; George Sheldon; Dudley Wolfe; 9 Sherpas	Second American Expedition Self-financed by expedition members; no oxygen equipment	Abruzzi Ridge route; Camp 8 at 7711 m; Camp 9 (assault camp) at 7940 m by the lowest rocks of summit pyramid; several members out of action; summit bid by Wiessner and Sherpa Pasang Dawa Lama reaches rocks of summit bulwark; descending Wolfe, Wiessner and Pasang find the chain of camps partially cleared; Wolfe and Sherpas Kikuli, Kitar and Pintso do not return.
7	1953	**Charles Houston**; Robert Bates; George Bell; Robert Craig; Art Gilkey; Dee Molenaar; Pete Schoening; Tony Streather	Third American Expedition Patron: American Alpine Club; no oxygen equipment	Abruzzi Ridge route; Art Gilkey taken seriously ill; multiple fall, Gilkey lost.
	1953	**Riccardo Cassin**	Italian Expedition Patron: Club Alpino Italiano	Reconnaissance

Year		Leader/Participants	Expedition/Organisation	Route/Remarks
8	1954	**Ardito Desio**; Erich Abram; Ugo Angelino; Walter Bonatti; Achille Compagnoni; Mario Fantin; Cirillo Floreanini; Pino Galotti; Lino Lacedelli; Guido Pagani; Mario Puchoz; Ubaldo Rey; Gino Solda; Sergio Viotto	Large Italian Expedition Patron: Club Alpino Italiano Finance: state, club Donations: 16 tons baggage, oxygen equipment	First ascent of K2 on 31 July by Lino Lacedelli and Achille Compagnoni by the Abruzzi Ridge; 9 camps and an assault tent at about 8050 m.
9	1960	**W. D. Hackett** (USA); Davis Bohn (USA); Ludwig Greissl (Ger.); Günther Jahr (Ger.); Lynn Pease (USA); Herbert Wünsche (Ger.)	Small American-German Expedition	Abruzzi Ridge, as far as Black Pyramid.
10	1975	**James Whittaker**	Large American Expedition	Attempt on a new route from Savoia Saddle.
11	1976	**Januscz Kurczab**; Leszek Cichy; Eugeniusz Chroback; Jan Holnicki-Szulc; Wojciech Wrz, and others	Large Polish Expedition Association of Polish Alpine Clubs; oxygen equipment	North-East Spur (first attempted by Oscar Eckenstein in 1902); two summit bids; on 15 August Chroback and Wrz failed at 8400 m.
12	1977	**Ichiro Yoshizawa**; total of 42 climbers, including: Mitsuoh Hirishima; Shoji Nakamura; Masahide Onodera; Tsuneho Shigehiro; Takeyoshi Takatsuka; Hideo Yamamato; film team	Mammoth Japanese Expedition Oxygen equipment; 1500 porters	Second Ascent K2 by Abruzzi Ridge; paramilitary leadership from Base Camp by radio and relay; 6 camps; 6 Japanese and 1 Pakistani reach summit on 8 and 9 August; all with oxygen.
13	1978	**James Whittaker**; total of 12 climbers including 2 women, amongst them: Louis Reichardt; Rick Ridgeway; John Roskelly; James Wickwire	Sixth American K2 Expedition Oxygen equipment taken	North-East Spur to about 7700 m, then traverse over East Shoulder to the Abruzzi Ridge route; four climbers reach summit on 7 and 8 August, 2 totally without oxygen.
14	1978	**Chris Bonington**; 8 climbers including 'veterans' of the British South-West Face of Everest-crew – including: Nick Estcourt; Jim Duff; Doug Scott; Pete Boardman; Paul Braithwaite	British Expedition No oxygen equipment	First attempt on West Ridge; after Nick Estcourt dies under avalanche, attempt called off.
15	1979	**Reinhold Messner** (Italy); Renato Casarotto (Italy); Michl Dacher (Ger.); Alessandro Gogna (Italy); Friedl Mutschlechner (Italy); Robert Schauer (Austria)	Small international expedition in alpine style; no oxygen equipment; self-financed	For reasons of safety, plans to attempt the 'Magic Line' on South Spur have to be abandoned; climb Abruzzi Ridge; 3 camps and one assault tent.
16	1979	**Bernard Mellet**; 14 climbers including Ivan Ghirardini; Yannick Seigneur	Large French Expedition Patron: President Giscard d'Estaing; 30 tons equipment; 1700–1300 porters	South Spur; between 7 August and 25 September 5 unsuccessful summit bids. Death of a high-level porter.
17	1980	Peter Boardman; Dick Renshaw; Doug Scott; Joe Tasker	Very small British Expedition, alpine style	3 climbers twice reached 7900 m on Abruzzí Ridge.

Sources

Quotations and source material in this book come, amongst others, from the following works:

ARDITO DESIO, *Ascent of K2, Second Highest Peak in the World*, Elek (London, 1955)
G. O. DYHRENFURTH, *Baltoro – ein Himalaya-Buch*, Benno Schwabe & Co. Verlag (Basel, 1939)
G. O. DYHRENFURTH, *To the Third Pole, the History of the High Himalaya*, Werner Laurie (London, 1955)
TOM LONGSTAFF, *This My Voyage*, John Murray (London, 1950)
GALEN ROWELL, *In the Throne Room of the Mountain Gods*, Sierra Club Books (San Francisco, 1977)
FRITZ WIESSNER, *K2 – Tragödien und Sieg am zweithöchsten Berg der Erde*, Bergverlag Rudolf Rother (Munich, 1955)
SIR FRANCIS YOUNGHUSBAND, *Everest The Challenge*, Thomas Nelson (London, 1936)

Der Spiegel, No. 28-31/1979

Private diaries of the expedition members

Data for the sketch panorama pages 6/7 from the book *Trekking in the Himalayas* by Tomoya Iozawa

Picture Acknowledgements

All colour pictures placed at our disposal by members of the 1979 K2-Expedition. Black/white illustrations are drawn from the private archives of Reinhold Messner, as well as from expedition members and also historical pictures from earlier K2-expeditions.
For permission to use documentary picture material the author and publishers wish to thank in particular: Ardito Desio (Milan), Deutscher Alpenverein (Munich), Dr Charles Houston (Burlington), Pervez A. Khom (Lahore), Dianne Roberts (Seattle), Galen Rowell (Albany) as well as the archive Vittorio Sella (Biella).

Traced from a sketch taken on the spot by Colonel Godwin Austen who first surveyed

x This point is 15 miles from the foot of the glacier